Kathleen Thorne-Thomsen   Hildy Paige Burns   A

For M.B.S. and Freestone

Special thanks to Judi Burns and Mary Thorne-Thomsen for their valuable editorial assistance; to Lynn Boscoe, Steve Burns, Richard Burns, John Thorne-Thomsen and Ross Carron for their much appreciated help; and to James Augustyn, Nannette Cameron, Jill Disney, Sandy Gordon, Catherine Harwood, Diane Hesley, Mimi Jasinsky, James Kidder, Mary Knowles, Bruce Kortebien, S. Magnolia, Bruce Montgomery, Darcy Paige, Caryn Schreiber, Nancy Lou Tate, Sara Thorne-Thomsen, and Anne Wilson for their contributions. Special thanks also to Ilse and Albert Wiener of Handcraft From Europe for their technical assistance. Without the time, talent, and concern so generously offered by these people this book would not have been possible.

COVER:
PENNSYLVANIA DUTCH CHURCH SAMPLER

Copyright © 1974 by Litton Educational Publishing, Inc.
Library of Congress Catalog Card Number 73-10746

ISBN 0-442-22612-8

Designed by the authors

Paperback published in 1980 by
Van Nostrand Reinhold Company
A Division of Litton Educational Publishing, Inc.
135 West 50th Street, New York, N.Y. 10020

16   15   14   13   12   11   10   9   8   7   6   5   4

Alphabetical Listing of Patterns

Color Plates

Introduction

The cross-stitch has long been one of the most versatile and widely used stitches in American embroidery. In the very simplicity of the stitch lies much of its charm—one stitch crossed over another again and again in neat geometric rows to form delicate patterns, figures, and pictorial scenes. Although European in origin, cross-stitching is now an integral part of American folk art. Being one of the few possessions small enough to carry along on the crowded ships, and essential to the making and repair of clothing, needle and thread were brought to America. Young ladies were taught the art of embroidery as part of their basic education, and cross-stitch was one of the earliest lessons and favored stitches. Girls were expected to be accomplished in the art of stitchery by marriageable age.

The art of cross-stitching has flourished throughout the many periods of American history, and today's renaissance in handwork has rekindled interest in the rich heritage of American cross-stitch design. American Cross-Stitch is a collection of patterns inspired by this heritage, as well as by the legends, folklore, and Americana that our culture comprises. Expression through stitchery is a highly individual matter, one which should be both pleasurable and rewarding. There are no rules governing the application of cross-stitch nor are there definite guidelines for the methods, materials, and colors to be used.

The information given here regarding the fabrics, threads, and yarns is therefore merely a departure point, included by the authors with the hope that these suggestions will serve to expand, not limit, the possibilities for creative expression through cross-stitching.

We urge our readers to explore the varieties of materials available, to make use of the expertise of the needlecraft merchants, and to draw upon their own tastes and talents in pursuing the art of cross-stitching.

Materials for cross-stitching are available in a great many textures, colors, weights, and sizes. The multitude of threads and fabrics offers a wide variety of effects from the most subtle and delicate to the boldest and most colorful.

The numerous fabrics manufactured specifically for cross-stitching are composed of small woven squares which form a guide for the placement of stitches. The gauge of the fabric, or number of squares per inch, determines the size of the stitch. Among the fabrics available to the stitcher are:

Aida Cloth

This is a basketweave cloth available in two textures, regular Aida being the coarser and Pearl Aida being the finer weave. This material is most readily available in white and natural. Some mills also distribute Aida cloth in a variety of colors. This fabric has corner holes to facilitate placement of the needle. The color plates on page 55 were stitched on regular Aida cloth, and the plates on page 50 on Pearl Aida.

Hardanger Cloth

This is an evenly woven cloth with two warp threads and two weft threads. It is found in various gauges and colors, although it is most commonly available in white and natural. The weave of this cloth forms squares for guiding the stitches but lacks the corner holes of Aida.

Rug Canvas

Also referred to as Quickpoint, this material is available in various gauges in either cotton or bleached jute. Cotton rug canvas is an excellent choice for patterns covering an entire cloth. Bleached jute is the more suitable for spot patterns since its texture is attractive and the cloth softens with repeated washing. The color plates on page 53 were stitched on bleached jute rug canvas.

Penelope Canvas

This stiff canvas is found in assorted gauges, some with evenly spaced blue threads to act as stitching guides. By serving as a grid that can be removed after stitching is completed, the chief application of penelope canvas is to apply patterns to fabrics which are not suitable for cross-stitching. To use this technique, baste onto the fabric a piece of penelope canvas cut slightly larger than the pattern. Then stitch the pattern directly over the penelope canvas. When the stitching is completed, the canvas is removed by dampening the area and pulling each of the canvas threads from under the stitching.

Other Fabrics

Fabrics such as linen, wool, and cotton, found in a great variety of colors and textures, may be used successfully in cross-stitching as long as they have an evenly spaced weave (i.e., the same number of warp and weft threads). If penelope canvas is not used for transferring the pattern, thread-count embroidery may be used. As the name implies, this is a method of counting the threads to determine the size of the square. This method is time consuming and requires meticulous work but affords an expanded range of fabrics on which to stitch.

As with the fabrics, the threads and yarns available offer an array of colors, textures, and weights from which to choose. A myriad of effects can be achieved by taking advantage of the many different threads and yarns. It is advisable to keep in mind the nature of the fabric being used when choosing threads and yarns. Wools are best with heavy or coarse fabrics. Cottons and linens are best for fine, close weaves.

Wool
Two excellent wools to choose from are tapestry wool and Persian wool. Tapestry wool is four ply; Persian wool is three strands of two ply.

Six Strand Cotton Embroidery Floss
This J. P. Coats thread was used to color code the patterns in this book because it is easily available in most variety stores. This thread is best used on finer weaves and where durability is not a prime factor. The six strands are easily separated, if fewer than six strands are desired for stitching.

Pearl Cotton
A mercerized cotton is available in numbers 3, 5, and 8, number 8 being thinner than number 3. It has a high sheen and a tight twist, which when stitched, gives a pearly effect.

Retors A Broder
This is a relatively heavy matte cotton. It is slightly thicker than number 3 pearl cotton. It gives a wool-like effect but is more practical than wool because it is easily washable.

Linen Floss
A two-strand embroidery floss, linen floss is slightly thicker than cotton and is more durable. It is therefore a good thread to use on more substantial fabrics.

The Stitchery
204 Worcester Turnpike
Wellesley Hills, Mass. 02181

Boutique Margot
26 West 54th Street
New York, N. Y. 10019

Selma's Art Needlework
1645 2nd Avenue
New York, N. Y. 10028

The Swedish Style Knitting Shop
5209 North Clark Street
Chicago, Ill. 60640

Maribee
Department B-77
2904 West Lancaster
Fort Worth, Tex. 76107

The Handweaver
111 East Napa Street
Sonoma, Cal. 95476

Handcraft From Europe
P.O. Box 372
Store: 1201 Bridgeway Blvd.
Sausalito, Ca. 94965

Binding the edges of the fabric before proceeding with the embroidery prevents the fabric from unraveling and may be accomplished by taping or making overcasting stitches around the outer edges of the cloth. To ensure that the yarn or thread gives the desired coverage on the fabric, stitch a test swatch. A 10 x 10 stitched square is sufficient.

All of the patterns in this book have been designed on a ten-square grid. The size of the finished stitched pattern is governed by the size of the square in the fabric used. For example, if a fabric with fifteen squares per inch is selected, the finished pattern will be smaller than it appears in the book. It will be larger if a five-square-per-inch fabric is used.

To ensure the proper placement of the pattern design on the fabric to be stitched, locate and mark its center. This may be done by basting two lines, one vertical and one horizontal, through the center point. Then the stitching can begin, working outward toward the borders.

Another method for pattern placement is achieved by basting a grid which corresponds to every ten squares in the pattern grid. The pattern can be transferred square by square and errors detected easily. If the pattern to be covered is completely filled with stitches, a light pencil sketch can provide a guide for stitching.

The borders of the completed needlework may be turned under and hemmed with a blind stitch. Turning the hem up and making a colorful border of crosses or another favorite stitch can also produce an attractive finishing touch.

The finished cross-stitch piece should be pressed by placing a towel above and beneath the fabric and ironing lightly with steam. If the pressed needlework does not lie smooth and flat, it should be blocked. To block, soak the cloth in cold water and Woolite and roll the cloth in a towel to extract the excess moisture. Do not wring or squeeze. Cover a half-inch plywood board with Contact paper to prevent the wood from staining the fabric. Tack the corners and sides of the fabric to the board with 1½″ galvanized nails. Allow it to dry and remove the flattened cloth.

To begin the stitch, the needle is brought up from the underside of the fabric through the lower left hole in a square. It is reinserted in the corner hole diagonally across from it, forming the first half of the cross-stitch. The needle is brought up again through the lower right hole of the square, and is reinserted in the remaining hole, the hole diagonally across from it. This forms a single cross. Repeating the stitch in this fashion maintains a uniform texture.

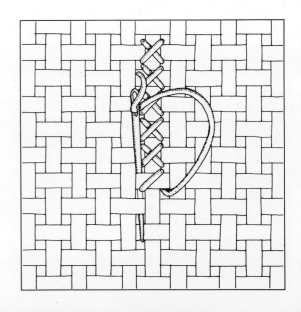

Cross-Stitch: Filling Stitch

Outline Stitch

French Knot

Useful in filling large areas of one color, the filling stitch is begun by making the first half of each cross-stitch progressing upward in a row from the bottom to the top. The needle is brought up from the underside of the fabric through the lower right hole of a square, and is reinserted in the upper left hole. The upward succession of these single stitches is made until the desired number is reached. The needle then returns down the row from the top to the bottom, forming the second half of the cross-stitch. To make these returning stitches, the needle is brought up from the underside of the canvas through the upper right hole and is reinserted in the lower left hole in each square. This method of cross-stitching also produces vertical rows of parallel stitches on the reverse side of the fabric.

To start the stitch, the needle is brought up from the underside of the fabric through a hole. It is then reinserted downward through the fabric one hole forward. The needle is then returned to the hole through which it first entered the fabric and brought back up through this hole, advanced two holes forward and reinserted downwards through the fabric. It is drawn up through the fabric one hole back at the point where the first stitch ended. Repeating the forward-two-holes, back-one-hole sequence, a line can be stitched in any direction.

The needle is brought up from the underside of the fabric, not through a hole but through a thread. The thread is pulled through and held taut between the thumb and forefinger of the hand not holding the needle. The needle is turned upward, away from the fabric directly under the fingers holding the thread, and the thread is wrapped one to three times around the needle depending on the desired weight of the knot. The needle is then turned down again and reinserted next to, not in the place where it first emerged. The thread is held taut while the needle and excess thread are slowly pulled through the cloth to form the knot.

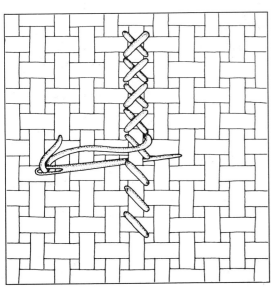

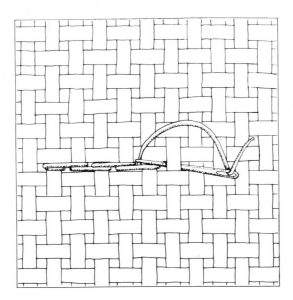

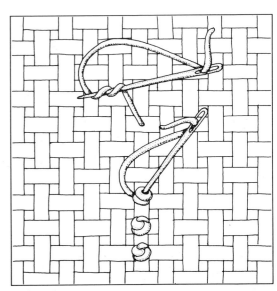

Pennsylvania Dutch Church Sampler

Suggested fabric: Aida cloth

- ■ Fast Red 100
- ◉ Gold Brown 51-C
- ☒ China Blue 76
- ◎ Sun Gold 223
- ◩ Avocado 216
- ▨ Grass Green 99
- ☐ Tangerine 38-B
- ⊞ Bright Gold 90-A

Outline stitch in windows and clock, Fast Red French knot stitch for eyes in angels, China Blue French knot stitch for eyes in birds, Sun Gold

**Pennsylvania Dutch
Star Sampler**
Suggested fabric: Aida cloth

- ■ Signal Red   140
- ▨ Steel Blue   108
- ⊡ Gold Brown   51-C
- ⊠ Avocado   216
- ◖ Bright Gold   90-A
- ◉ Tangerine   38-B
- ▨ Orange   11

11

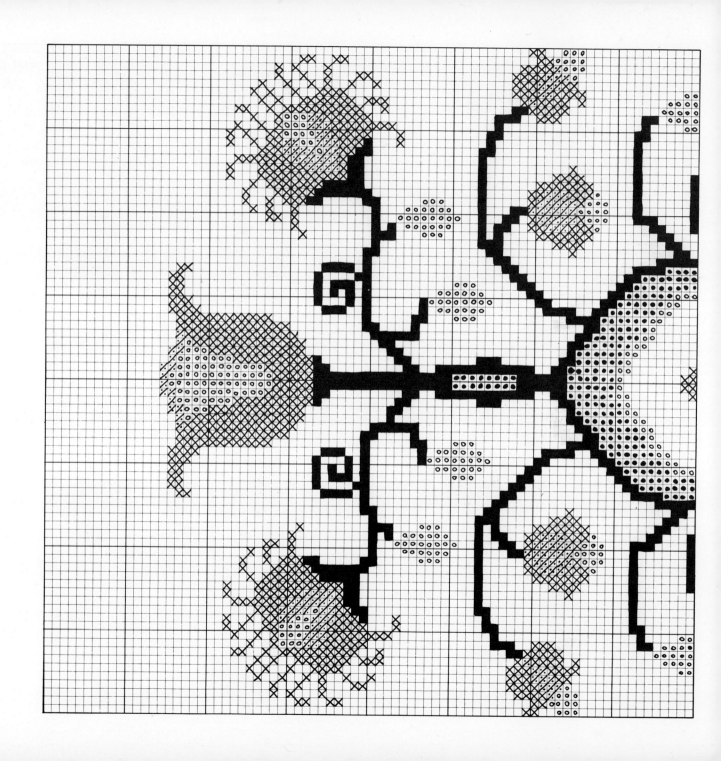

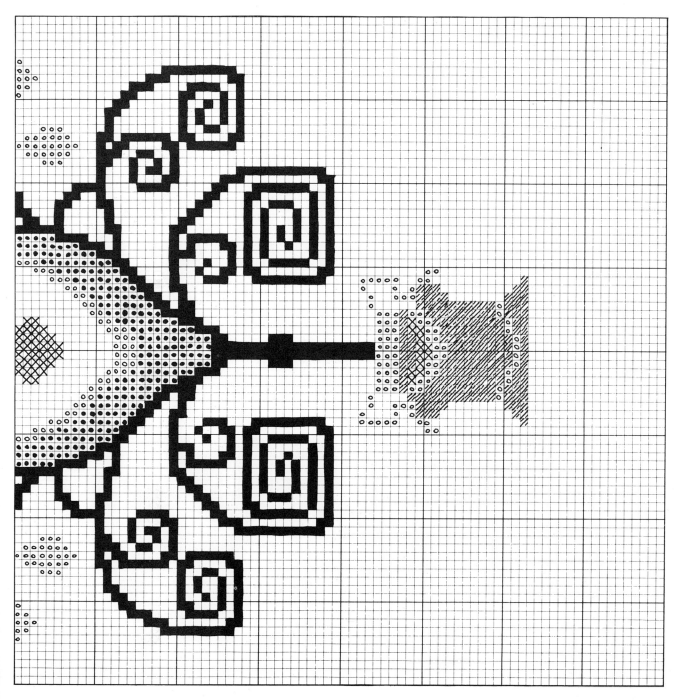

Pennsylvania Dutch Bouquet

Suggested fabric: Aida cloth

- ⊡ Sun Gold   223
- ⊠ Dark Orange   38
- ⊠ Signal Red   140
- ■ Myrtle   28
- ⊡ Avocado   216
- ⊠ Royal Blue   44

**Pennsylvania Dutch
Wedding Hearts**

Suggested fabric: Aida
cloth

☒ Signal Red   140

■ Grass Green   99

☐ Sun Gold   223

☒ Myrtle   28

Outline stitch in flowers,
Signal Red

14

Pennsylvania Dutch Tulips

Suggested fabric: Aida cloth

■ Treeleaf Green 28-B

☒ Signal Red 140

⊡ Tangerine 38-B

▥ Dark Orange 38

⊙ Bright Gold 90-A

**Pennsylvania Dutch Bowl
of Flowers**
Suggested fabric: Aida
cloth
◩ Gold Brown   51-C
⊡ Bright Gold   90-A
⊠ Signal Red   140
⊡ Grass Green   99
■ Treeleaf Green   28-B

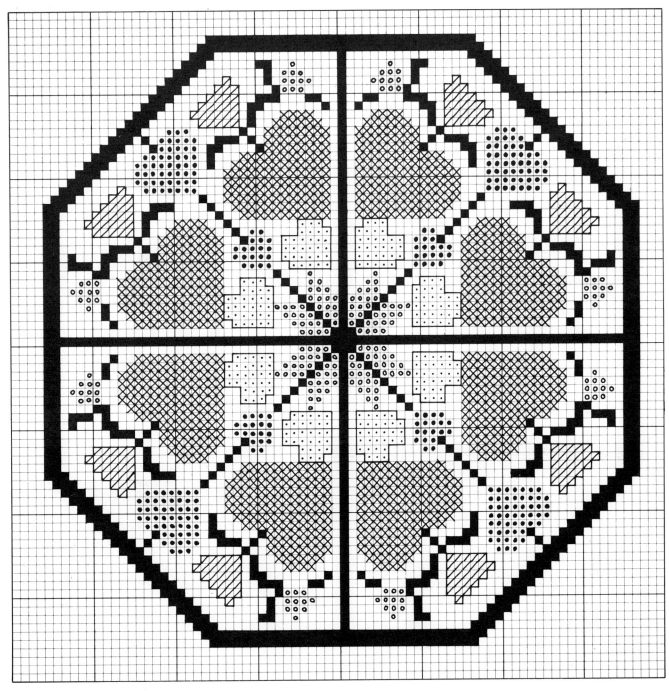

Pennsylvania Dutch Heart Sampler

Suggested fabric: Aida cloth

☒ Signal Red   140
◉ Deep Rose   59-A
⊡ Beauty Pink   65
◻ Light Steel Blue   69
◙ Dark Orange   38
■ Grass Green   99

Pennsylvania Dutch Drakes

Suggested fabric: Aida cloth

⊡ Fern Green   98
■ Treeleaf Green   28-B
⊠ Mid Rose   46-A
⊡ Deep Rose   59-A
⧄ Purple   32
⫼ Light Oriental Blue   24
⧄ Dark Oriental Blue   24-B

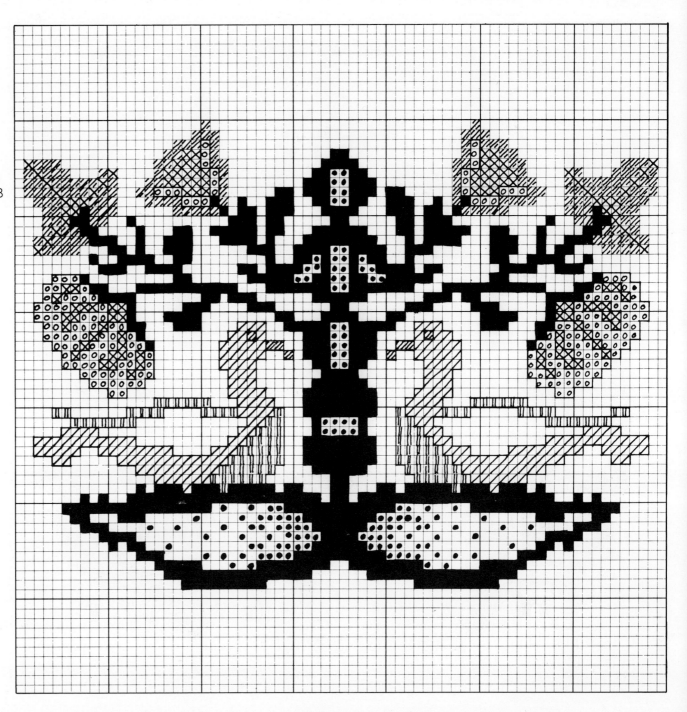

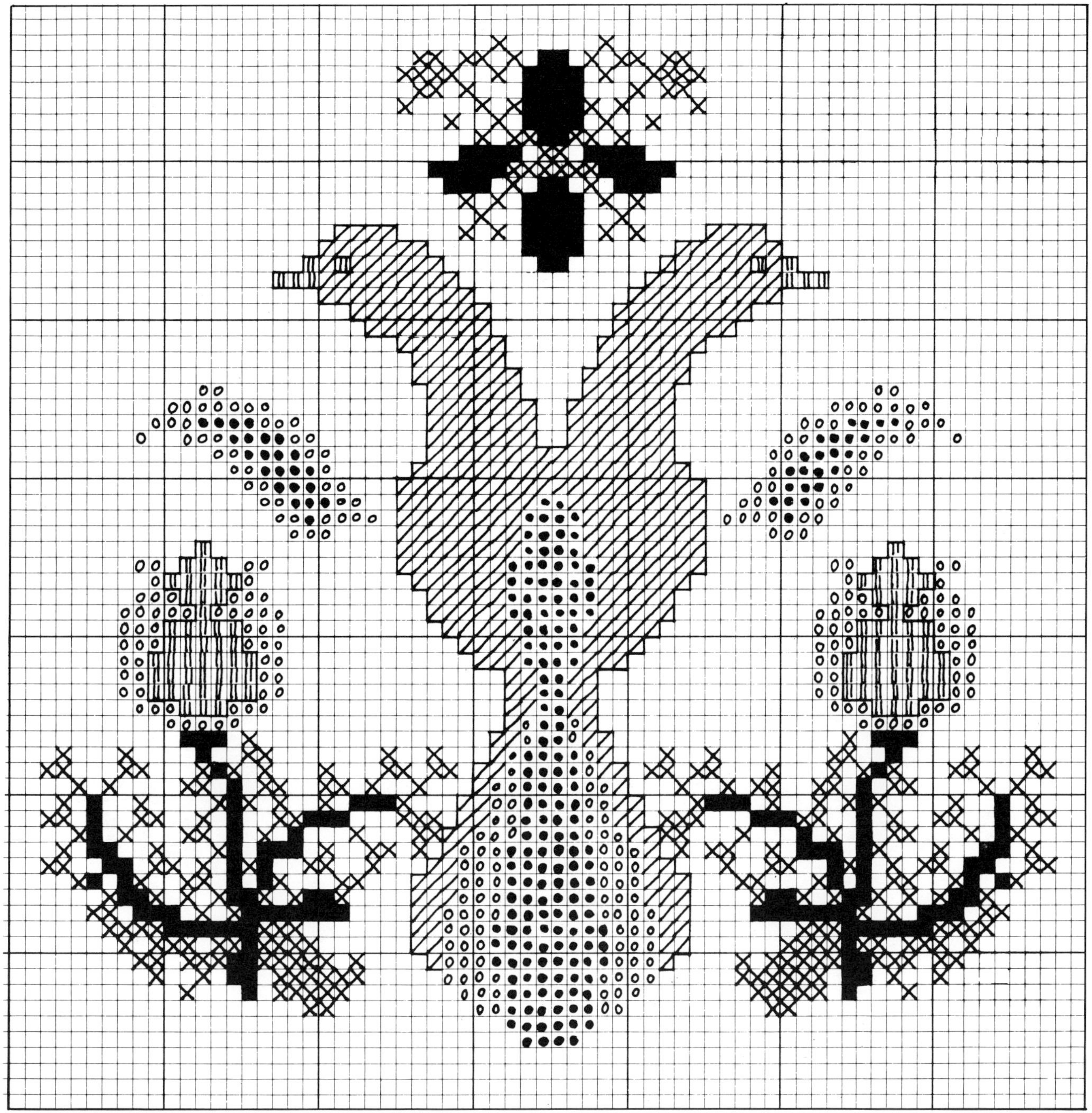

Pennsylvania Dutch Doves

Suggested fabric: Aida cloth

- ■ Dark Willow Green 109
- ⊠ Apple Green 215
- ◪ Bright Gold 90-A
- ▥ Dark Orange 38
- ◙ Tropic Orange 75-A
- ⊡ Fast Red 100

Pennsylvania Dutch Musicians

Suggested fabric: Aida cloth

⊡ Colonial Brown 81-A
◙ Gold Brown 51-C
◪ Charcoal 211
⊠ China Blue 76
■ Black 12
⊞ Indian Pink 124
◪ Bright Gold 90-A

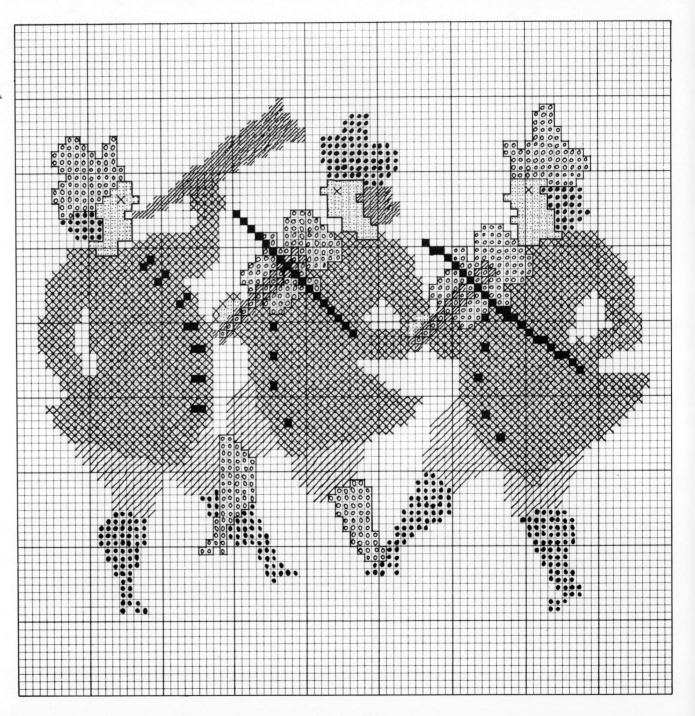

20

**Pennsylvania Dutch
Initial Heart**

Suggested fabric: Aida cloth

🗹 Russet 62
☒ Steel Blue 108
◉ Indian Pink 124
⦿ Signal Red 140
🗹 Bright Gold 90-A
■ Dark Hunter's Green
   48-A

Pennsylvania Dutch Borders

Suggested fabric: Aida cloth

⊠ Treeleaf Green   28-B
◙ Signal Red   140
◨ Dark Orange   38
⊡ Bright Gold   90-A
■ Avocado   216
Ⅲ Tropic Orange   75-A

Pennsylvania Dutch Quilting Pattern

Suggested fabric: Aida cloth

☒ Blue Iris   221

⊡ Ecru   61

Quilting Patterns

Pine Tree, upper left
Kansas Trouble, upper right
Lemon Star, lower left
Georgetown Circle, lower right
Suggested fabric: Aida cloth

⊙ Treeleaf Green 28-B
⊠ Royal Blue 44
◪ Tropic Orange 75-A
◩ Bright Gold 90-A
⊡ Blue Iris 221

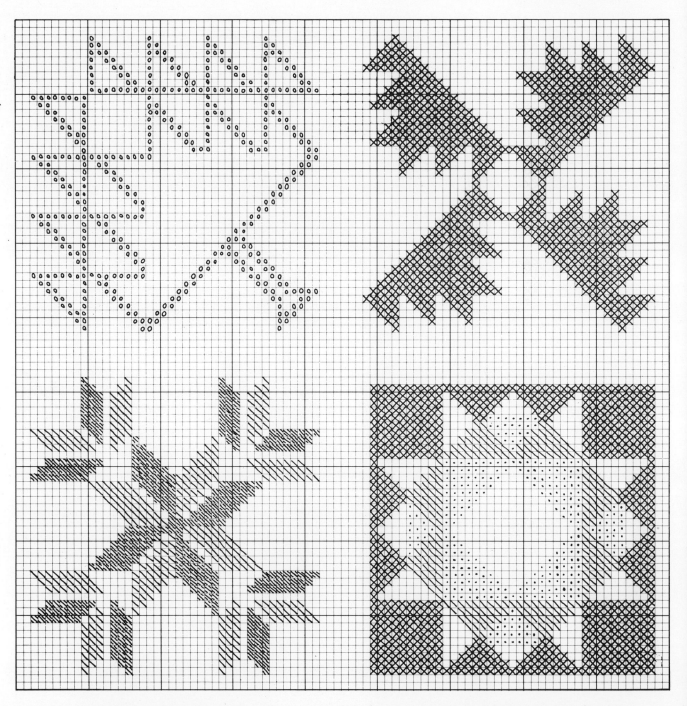

Missouri Star
Suggested fabric: Aida
cloth
☒ Sun Gold 223
⊡ Royal Blue 44

California Star

Suggested fabric: Aida cloth

☒ Steel Blue   108

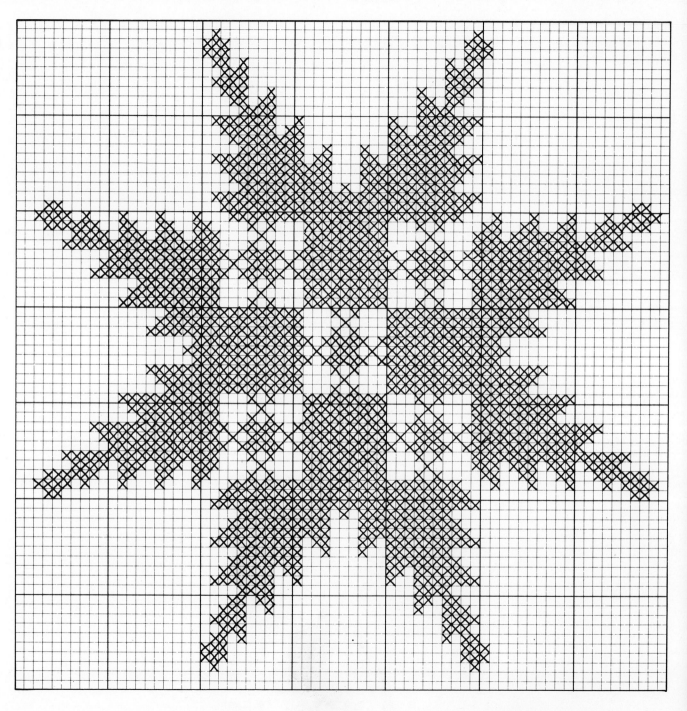

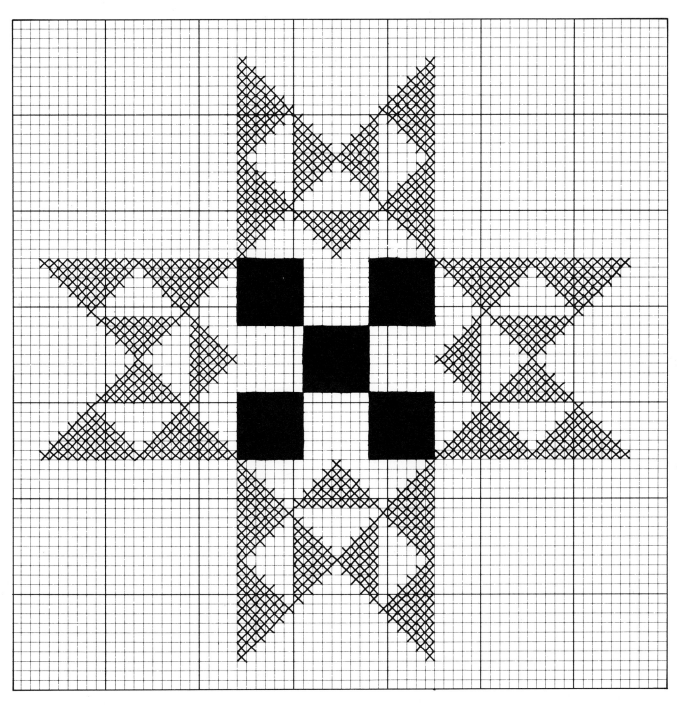

Dolly Madison
Suggested fabric: Aida cloth
■ Signal Red 140
⊠ Royal Blue 44

Boxes

Suggested fabric: Aida cloth

☒ Royal Blue 44
☐ Dark Rose 59-B

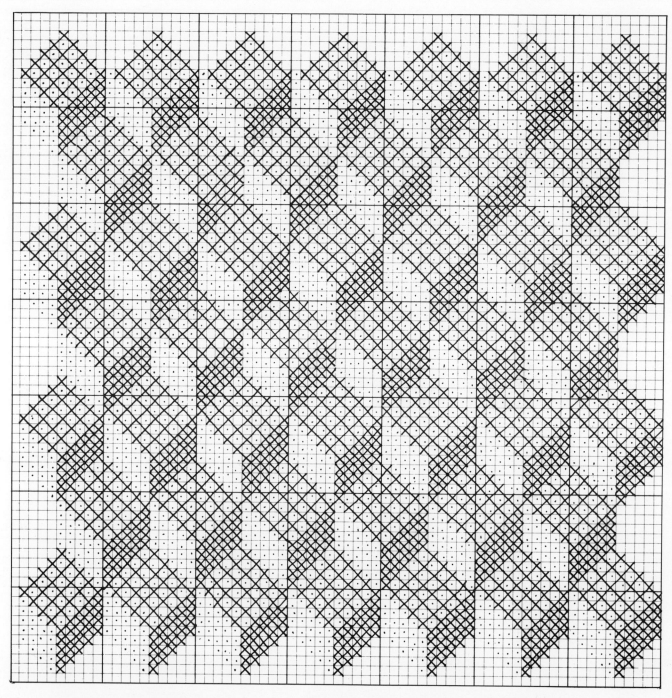

⊡ Russet 62
☑ Bright Gold 90-A
⊡ Dark Brown 81
⊠ Charcoal 211
◹ Royal Blue 44
☑ Tropic Orange 75-A
⊟ Warm Beige 214

Eight Block Pattern
Suggested fabric: rug
canvas
☐ Orange 11
⊡ Tangerine 38-B
■ China Blue 76

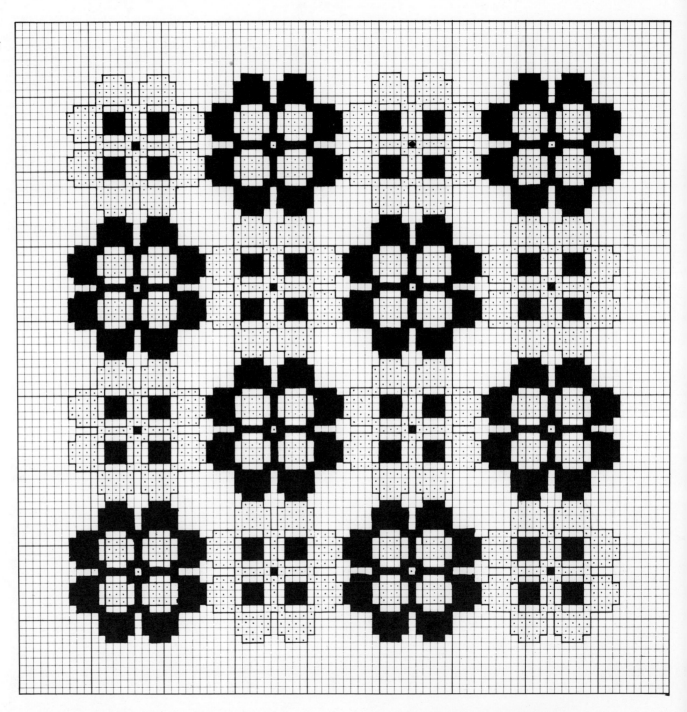

Suggested fabric: Aida
cloth or rug canvas
☒ Signal Red   140
■ Royal Blue   44

Stars and Stripes
Suggested fabric: Aida
cloth or rug canvas
☒ Signal Red   140
■ Royal Blue   44

Abraham Lincoln

Suggested fabric: Aida
cloth or rug canvas

☒ Beige 213
■ Black 12
☐ White 1
⊡ Indian Pink 124
Ⅲ Coral Glow 218
⊞ Pewter Grey 71

Outline stitch in face,
Black

George Washington
Suggested fabric: Aida
cloth or rug canvas
☒ Beige 213
■ Black 12
☐ White 1
⊡ Indian Pink 124
▥ Coral Glow 218
◪ Pewter Grey 71
Outline stitch in face,
Black

35

Liberty Bell Sampler

Suggested fabric: Aida
cloth

- ■ Steel Blue 108
- ⊠ Signal Red 140
- ⊡ White 1
- ◉ Bright Gold 90-A

Commemorative Eagle Sampler
Suggested fabric: Aida cloth
■ Steel Blue 108
⊠ Signal Red 140

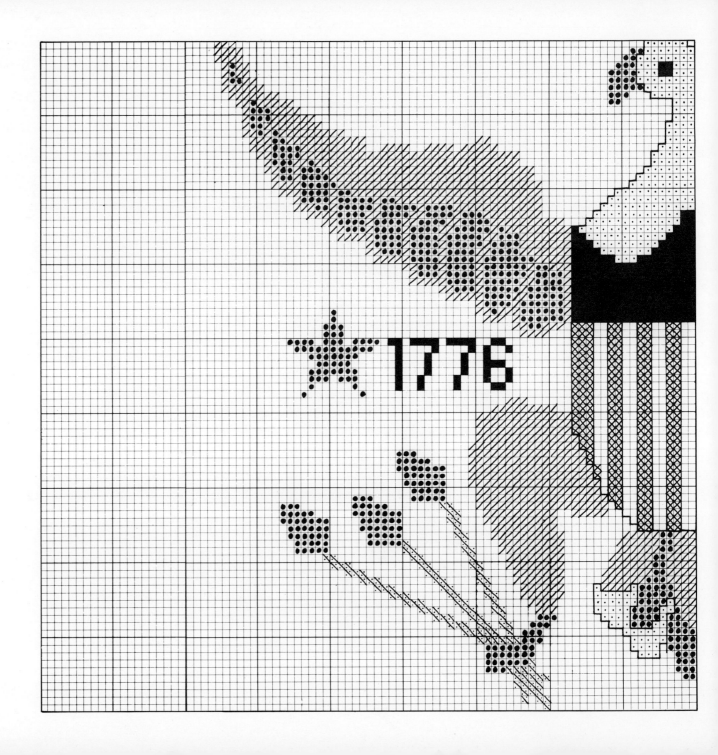

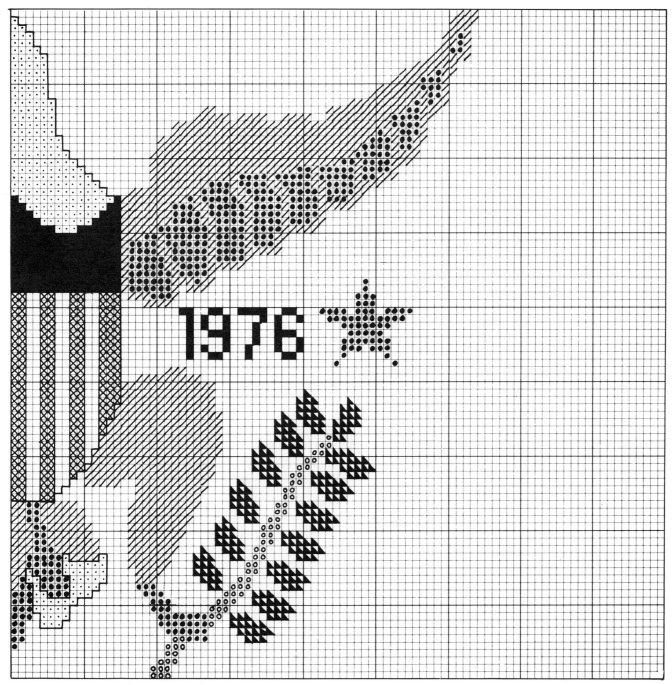

American Eagle

Suggested fabric: Aida cloth

- ■ China Blue 76
- ☒ Devil Red 141
- ▨ Dark Colonial Brown 81-B
- ⊡ Gold Brown 51-C
- ⊙ Bright Gold 90-A
- ◤ Avocado 216
- ◉ Treeleaf Green 28-B
- ◩ Dark Brown 81

Eagle
Suggested fabric: Aida
cloth
■ Royal Blue   44
☒ Signal Red   140

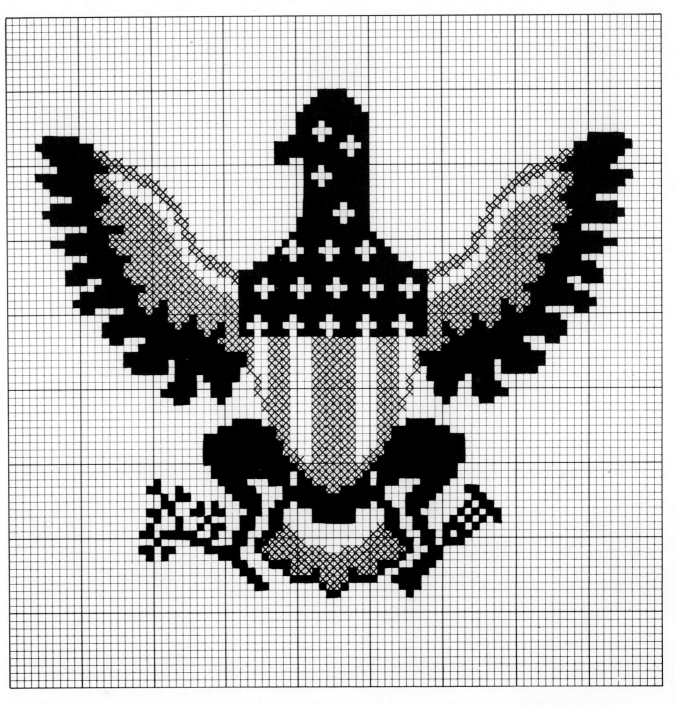

40

Uncle Sam
Suggested fabric: Aida cloth
■ China Blue   76
□ White   1
⊠ Signal Red   140
⊡ Indian Pink   124
⊞ Coral Glow   218
Ⅲ Crimson   120
◪ Silver Grey   70
Outline stitch in face and hand, China Blue

41

Mayflower Sampler

Suggested fabric: Aida cloth

- ■ Navy 55
- ◉ Dark Oriental Blue 24-B
- ☒ China Blue 76
- ◩ Oriental Blue 24-A
- ☑ Bright Gold 90-A
- ☐ Blue 8
- ⊡ Silver Grey 70

Outline stitch, Navy

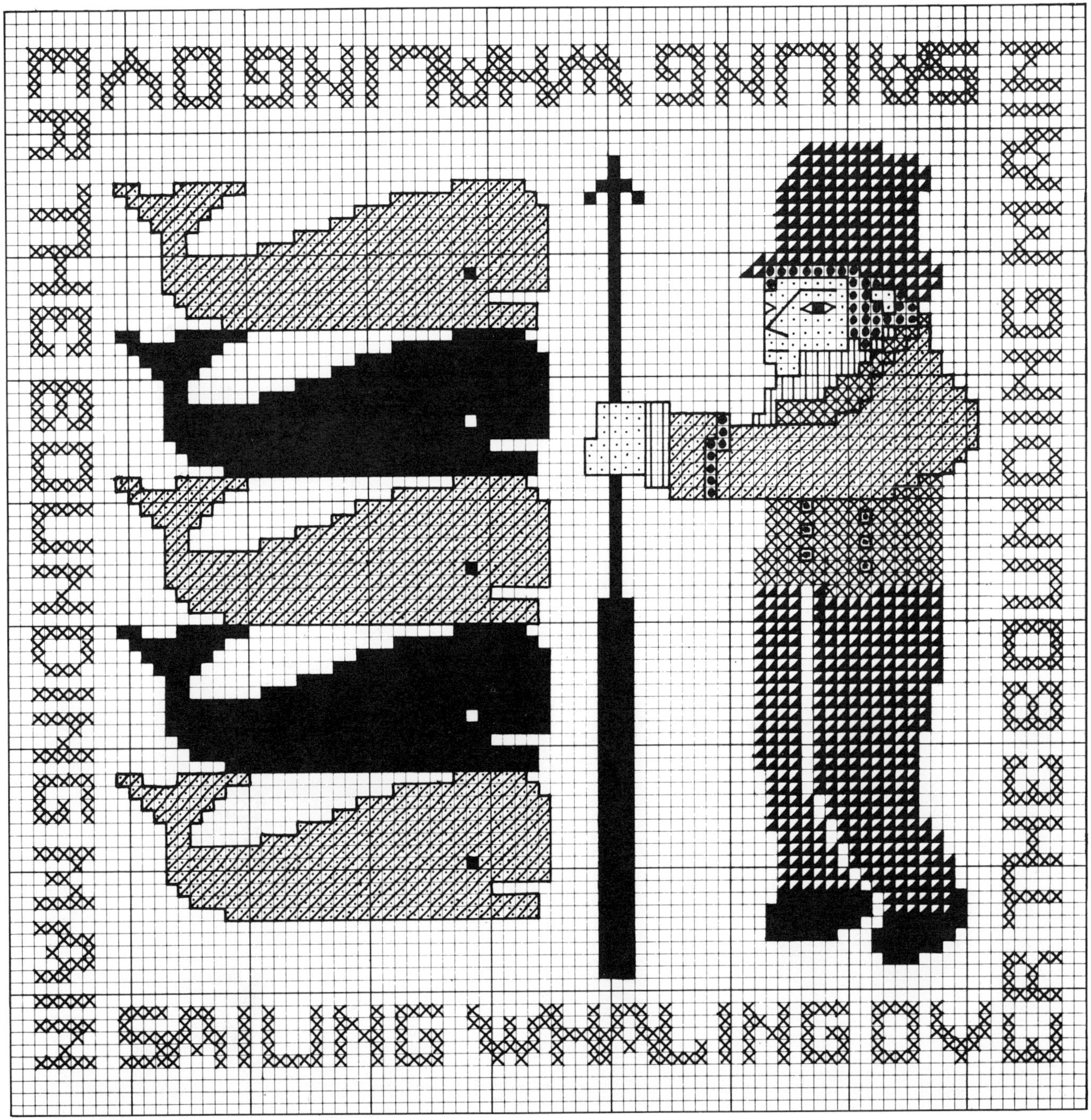

Sailing, Whaling

Suggested fabric: Aida cloth

- ⊘ Blue Iris 221
- ⊠ Royal Blue 44
- ◪ Navy 55
- ⊙ Bright Gold 90-A
- ⊡ Indian Pink 124
- ■ Pewter Grey 71
- ◫ Tangerine 38-B

Outline stitch in face, Navy

Whaling Ship

Suggested fabric: Aida
cloth or rug canvas

- ■ Royal Blue 44
- ⦚ Pewter Grey 71
- ⊙ Sun Gold 223
- ▨ Black 12
- ⊡ Signal Red 140
- ⊠ Steel Blue 108

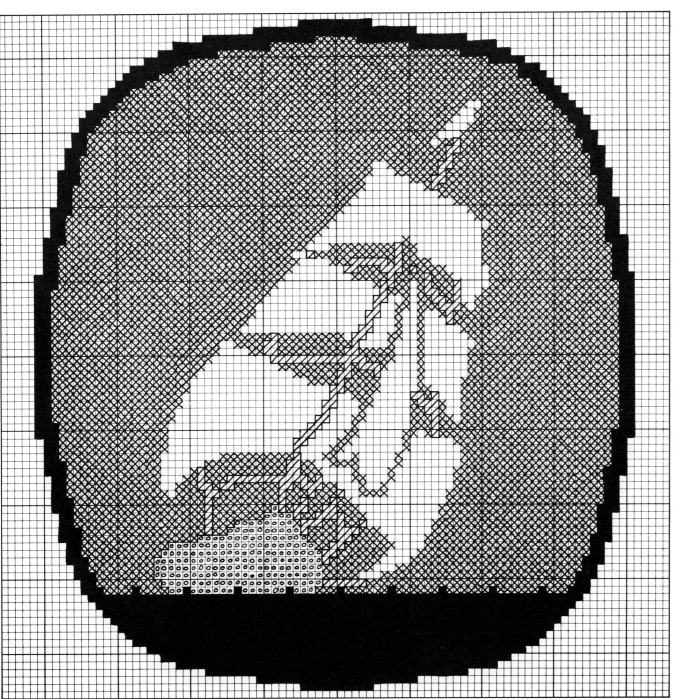

Clipper Ship
Suggested fabric: Aida
cloth or rug canvas
☒ Bluette 220
☑ Colonial Brown 81-A
☑ Black 12
■ Navy 55

New England Town

Suggested fabric: Aida cloth

- ⊙ Treeleaf Green 28-B
- ⊡ Blue Iris 221
- ■ Black 12
- ⊠ Dark Hunter's Green 48-A
- ▨ Grass Green 99
- ▨ Leaf Green 210

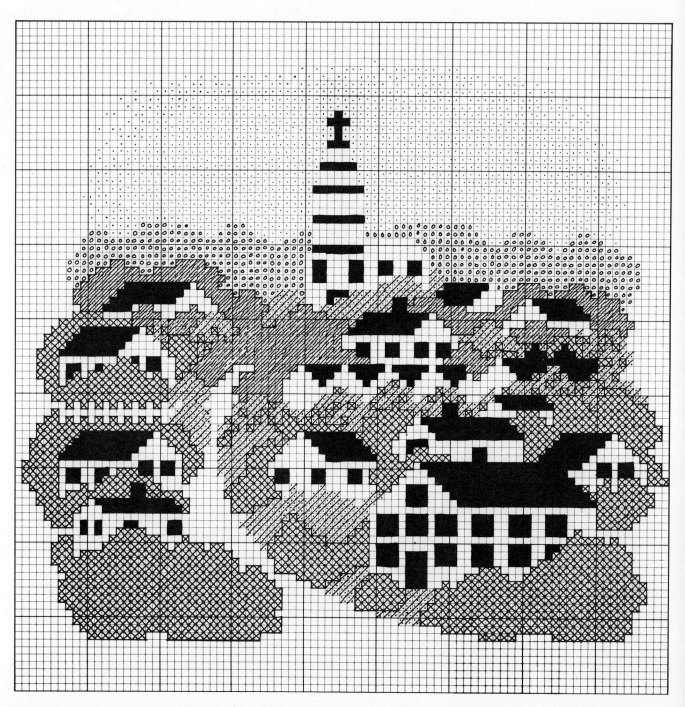

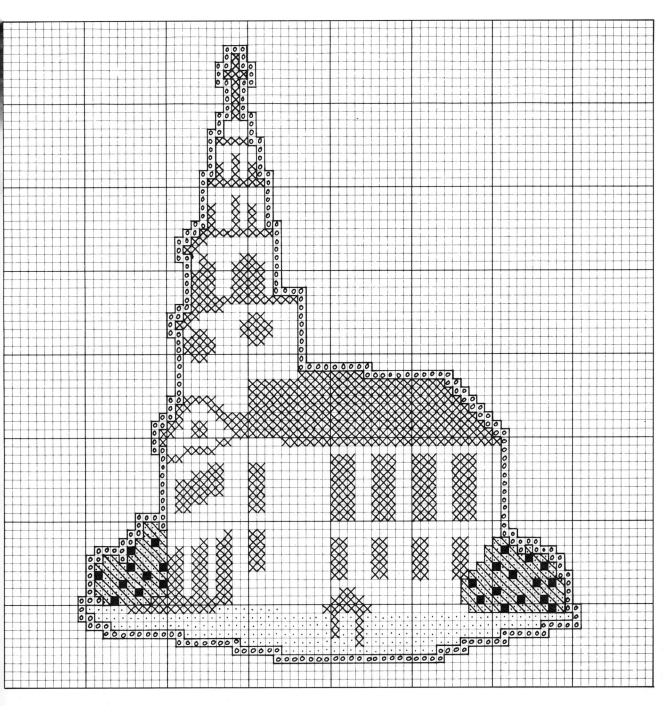

New England Church
Suggested fabric: Aida cloth

⊡ Grass Green   99
■ Signal Red   140
⊡ Blue Iris   221
⊠ Pewter Grey   71
⊠ Leaf Green   210

Hornbook Sampler

Suggested fabric: Aida cloth

- ■ Charcoal 211
- ☒ Blue Iris 221
- ▨ Avocado 216
- ◉ Mid Rose 46-A
- ⊡ Canary Yellow 10-A

George Washington   page 35

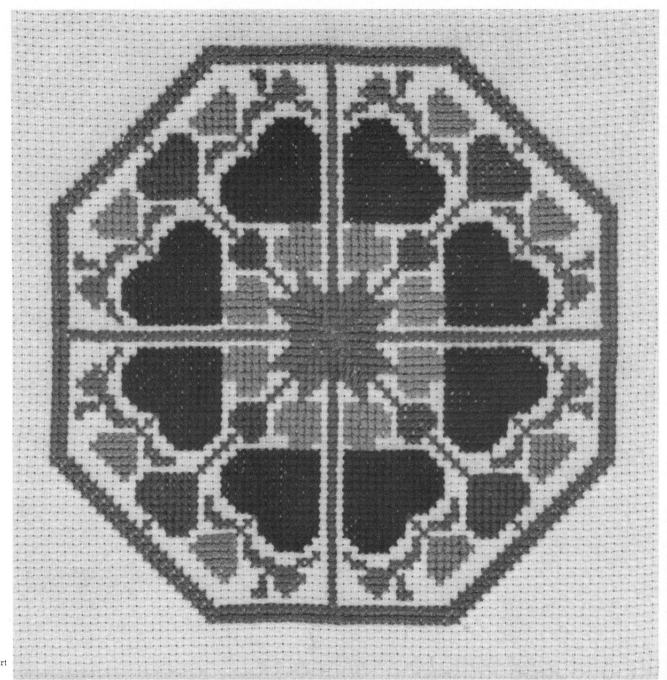

Pennsylvania Dutch Heart
Sampler page 17

Pennsylvania Dutch Quilting
Pattern   page 23

Quilting Pattern, Lemon Star
page 24

53

Be It Ever So Humble page 61

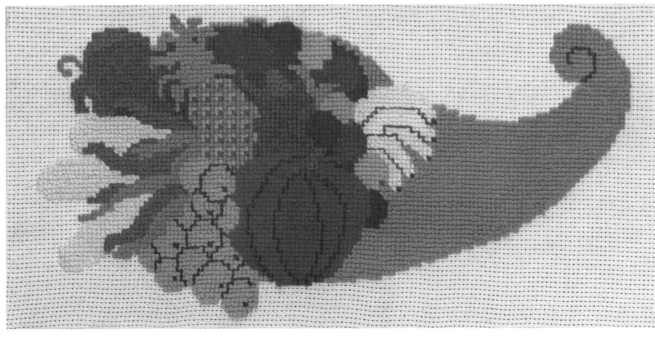

Gobbler page 58
American Tabby Cat page 60
Cornucopia page 62, 63

Homestead Sampler
Suggested fabric: Aida cloth

☒ Grass Green 99
☒ Steel Blue 108
◉ Dark Brown 81
◎ Deep Rose 59-A
☒ Tangerine 38-B
⊞ Dark Orange 38
☰ Pewter Grey 71
Ⅲ Fast Red 100
◉ Bright Gold 90-A
Ⅲ Purple 32
☑ Light Steel Blue 69
■ Myrtle 28

Gobbler

Suggested fabric: Aida cloth

- ■ Dark Colonial Brown 81-B
- ⊟ Tropic Orange   75-A
- ◪ Bright Gold   90-A
- ◉ Signal Red   140
- ◳ Dark Brown   81
- ⊠ Gold Brown   51-C
- ◉ Dark Willow Green 109
- ⊡ Ecru   61

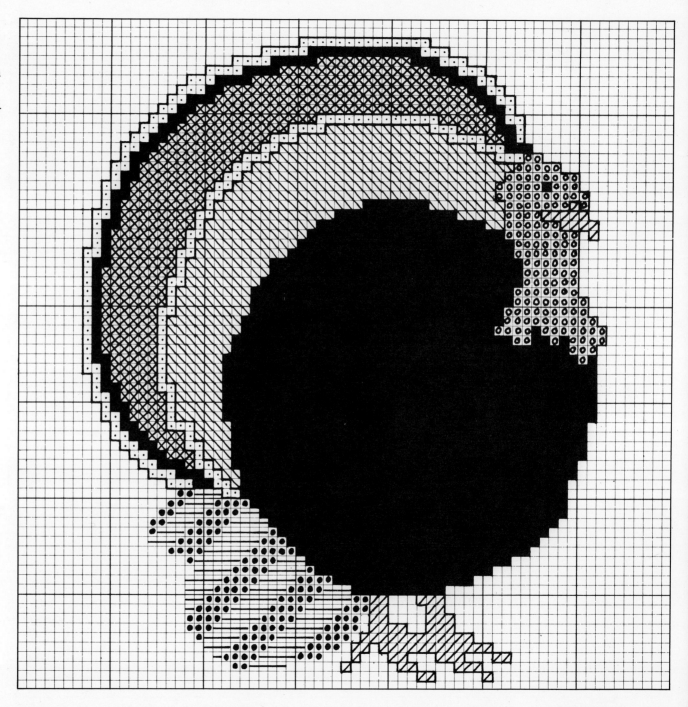

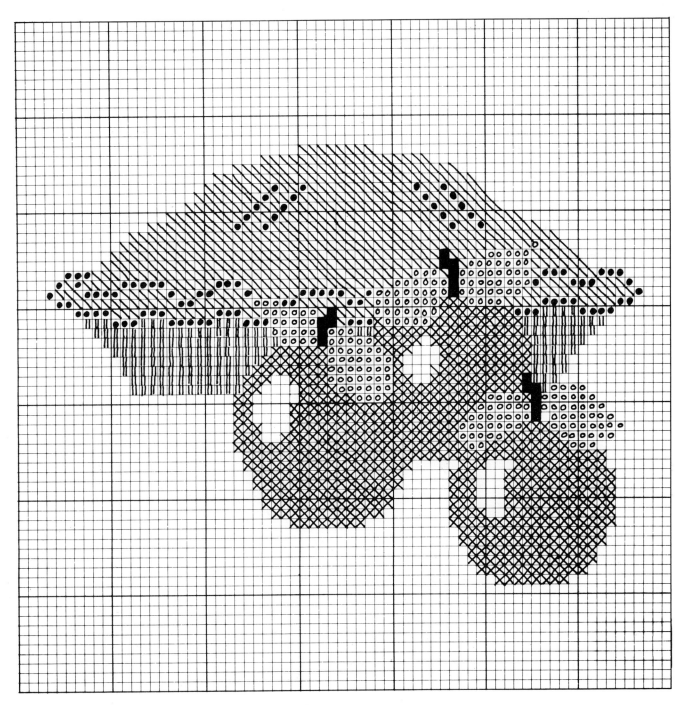

American Apple Pie
Suggested fabric: Aida cloth
⊡ Gold Brown 51-C
■ Colonial Brown 81-A
⊠ Signal Red 140
◨ Bright Gold 90-A
⊙ Myrtle 28
Ⅲ Pewter Grey 71

American Tabby Cat
Suggested fabric: Aida
cloth
■ Gold Brown 51-C
☒ Dark Colonial Brown
   81-B
⊡ Ecru 61
⊞ Avocado 216
◪ Coral Pink 217
⊘ Pastels 165

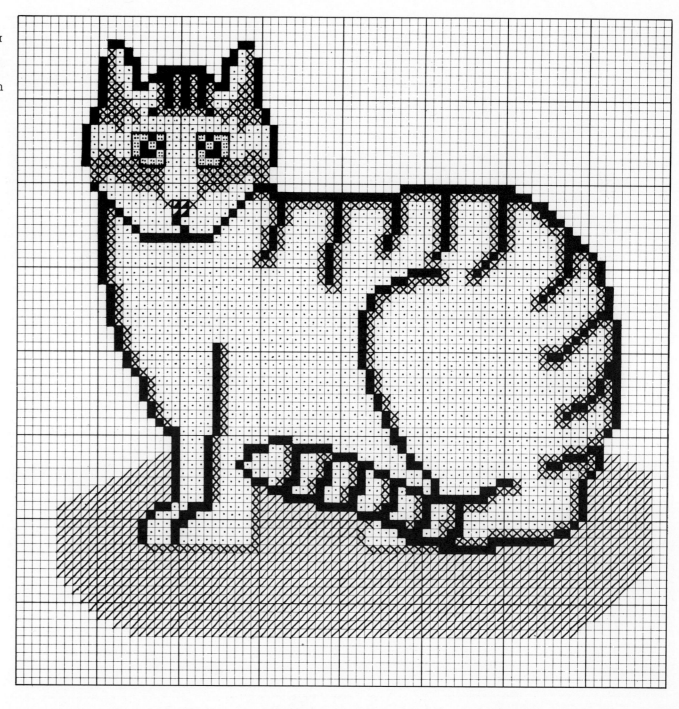

Be It Ever So Humble

Suggested fabric: Aida cloth

- ■ Russet 62
- ⊠ Royal Purple 36
- ⊙ Violet 54
- ⊿ Beauty Rose 46-B
- ⊡ Mid Pink 4-A
- ⊞ Blue Iris 221
- ⊡ Ecru 61
- ⊠ Avocado 216
- ◪ Dark Colonial Brown 81-B

Outline stitch in face, Dark Colonial Brown

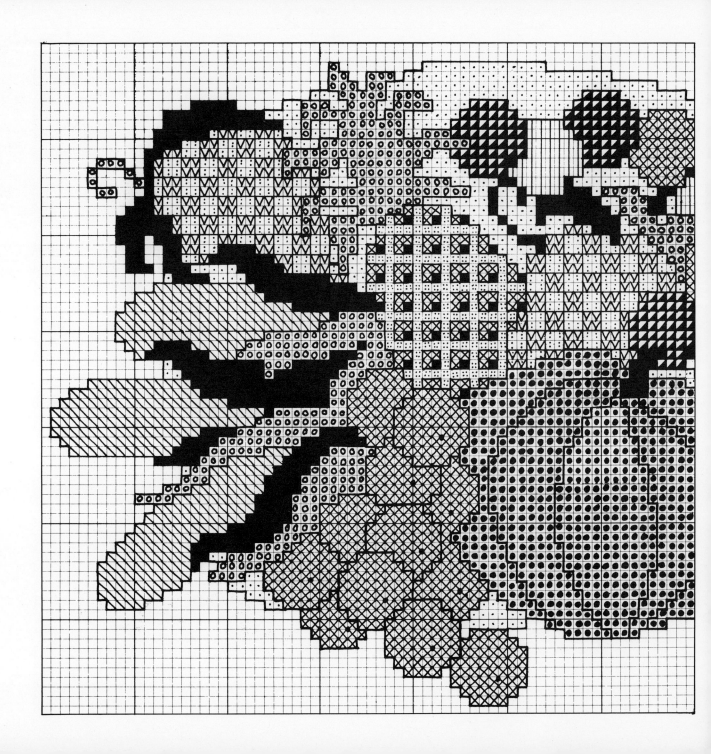

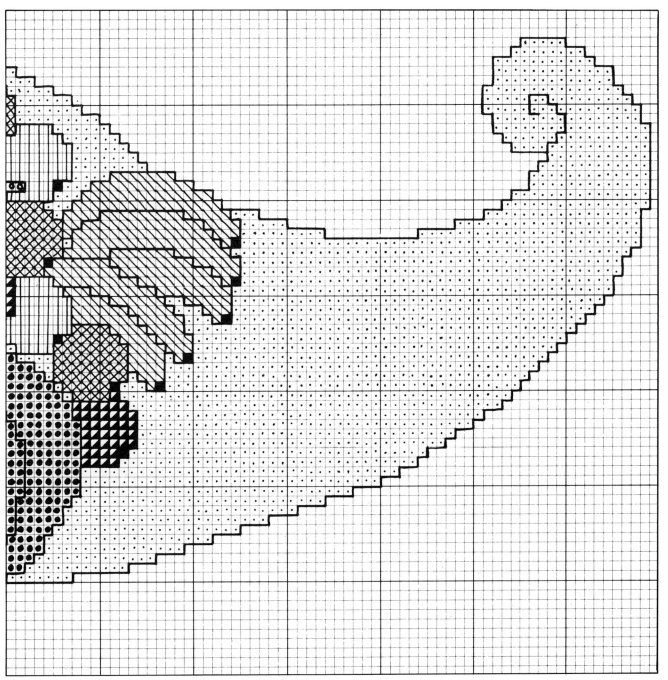

Cornucopia

Suggested fabric: Aida cloth

⊡ Bright Gold   90-A
⊠ Dark Orange   38
◩ Canary Yellow   10-A
■ Dark Willow Green   109
◙ Avocado   216
◩ Purple   32
⊡ Blue Iris   221
◪ Light Cardinal   143
⊓ Fast Red   100
⊞ Tropic Orange   75-A
◖ Tangerine   38-B

Outline stitch in oranges, pumpkin, apples, and bananas, Dark Willow Green

American Beauty Rose

Suggested fabric: Aida cloth or rug canvas

- ■ Royal Blue   44
- ⊠ Signal Red   140
- ▨ Fast Red   100
- ▢ Dark Hunter's Green 48-A

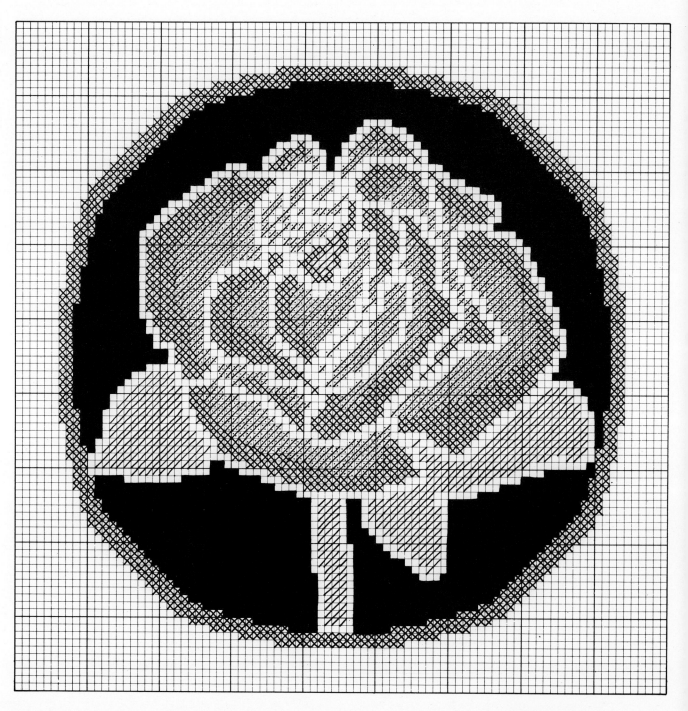

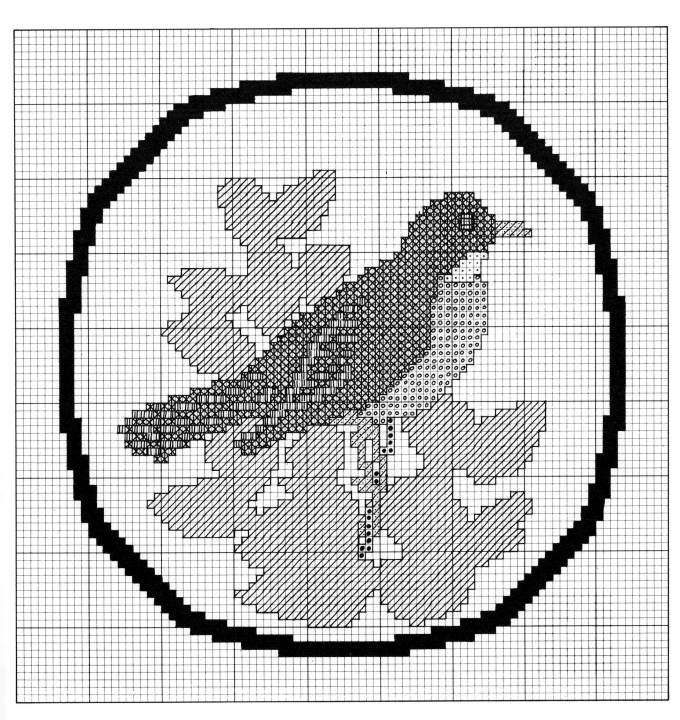

Robin Redbreast
Connecticut state bird
Suggested fabric: Aida
cloth or rug canvas
■ Myrtle 28
◪ Bright Gold 90-A
⫿⫿ Charcoal 211
⊞ Black 12
◉ Fast Red 100
⊡ Colonial Brown 81-A
◪ Grass Green 99
⊡ Ecru 61

Baltimore Oriole and Black-Eyed Susans

State bird and flower of Maryland
Suggested fabric: Aida cloth

- ■ Black 12
- ▨ Bright Gold 90-A
- ⊠ Tangerine 38-B

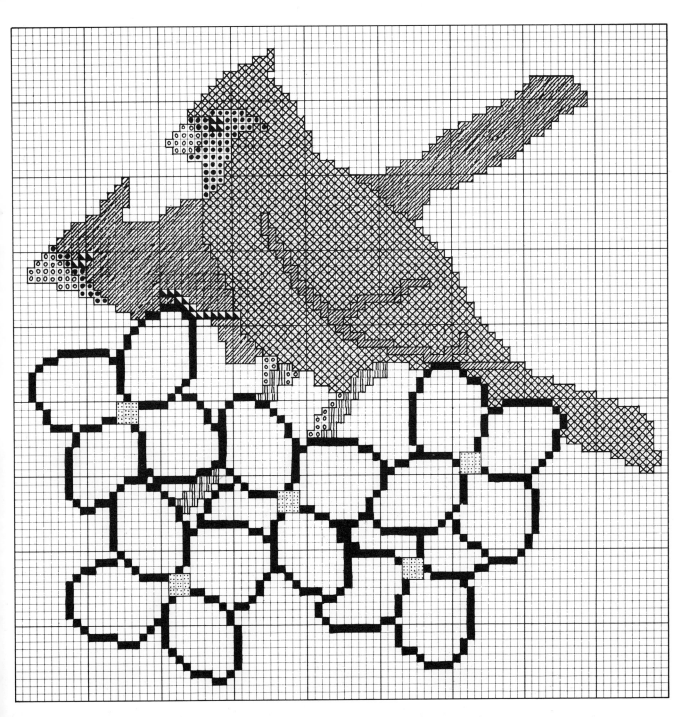

Cardinals and Dogwood Blossoms

State bird and flower of Virginia

Suggested fabric: Aida cloth

- ■ Coral Glow   218
- ⊡ Indian Pink   124
- ◉ Bright Gold   90-A
- ▨ Fast Red   100
- ⊙ Black   12
- ◣ Charcoal   211
- ⊠ Signal Red   140
- ⫿⫿⫿ Colonial Brown   81-A

Boston Baked Beans
Suggested fabric: Aida
cloth
⬚ Beige   213
◉ Gold Brown   51-C
☒ Colonial Brown   81-A
■ Signal Red   140
◉ Steel Blue   108

68

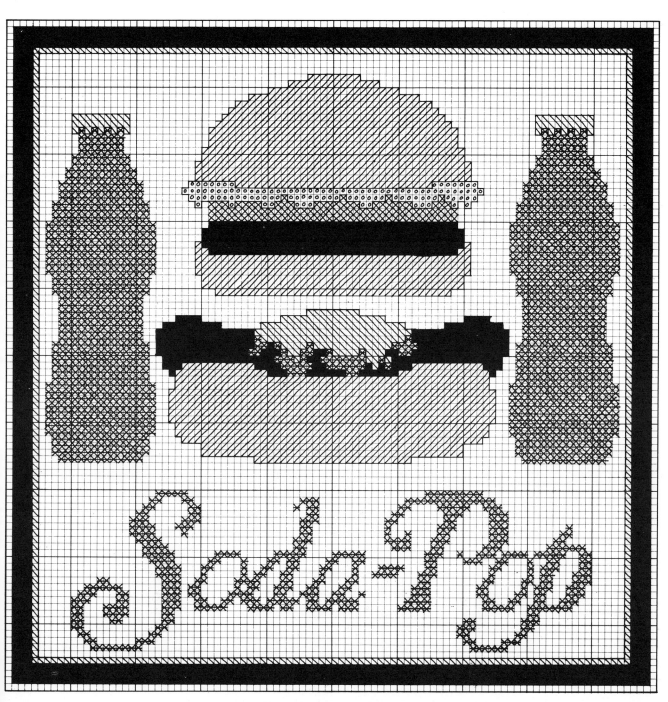

Soda-Pop Sampler

Suggested fabric: Aida cloth

☒ Signal Red   140
◻ Bright Gold   90-A
▨ Gold Brown   51-C
■ Colonial Brown   81-A
☒ Myrtle   28
⊡ Fern Green   98

Baseball Players

Suggested fabric: Aida cloth

⊡ Indian Pink 124
Ⅲ Charcoal 211
⊠ Fast Red 100
■ Dark Brown 81
◨ Silver Grey 70

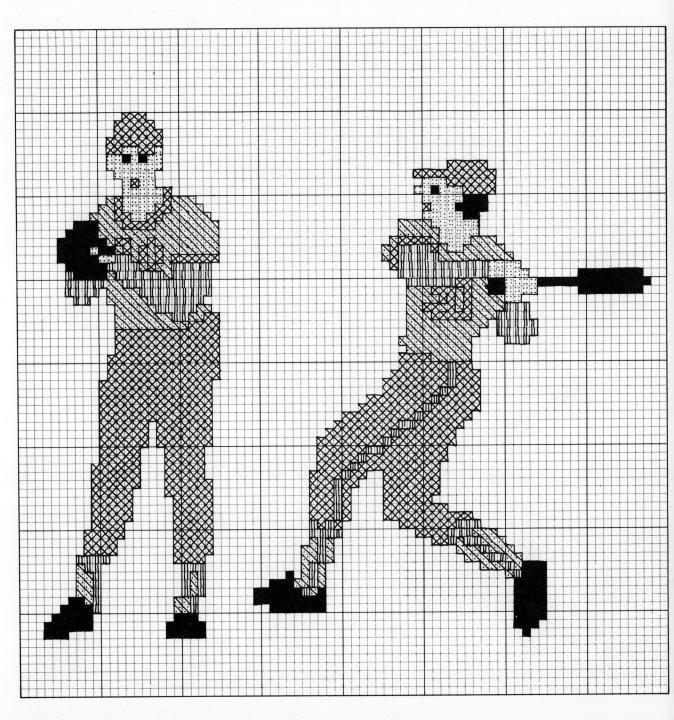

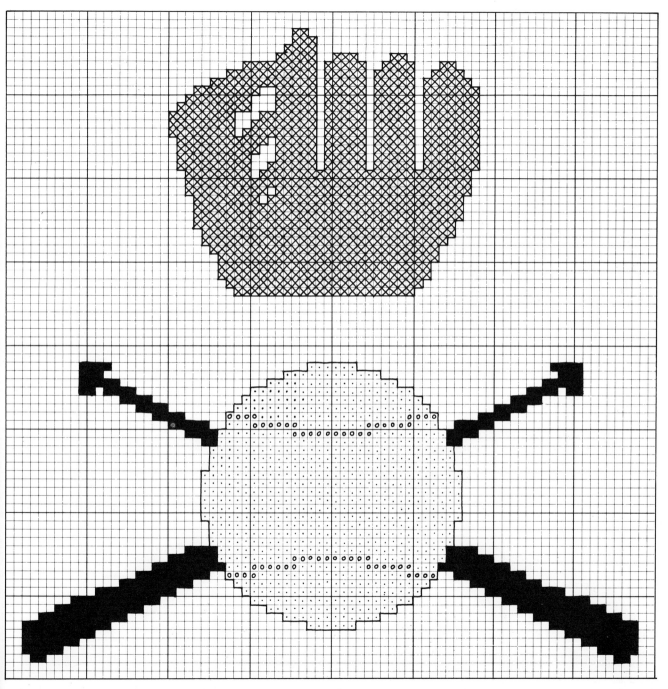

**Baseball Glove
Bat and Ball**
Suggested fabric: Aida
cloth
☒ Gold Brown   51-C
⊡ Beige   213
☉ Signal Red   140
■ Colonial Brown   81-A

**Circus Train (following
pages)**
Suggested fabric: Aida
cloth
■ Black   12
☒ Signal Red   140
◉ China Blue   76
◩ Pewter Grey   71
⊡ Orange   11
⊟ Grass Green   99
Ⅲ Gold Brown   51-C
◙ Bright Gold   90-A
◺ Indian Pink   124
◸ Tangerine   38-A
⊟ Colonial Brown   81-A
◩ Crimson   120
Outline stitch in smoke,
Black
Outline stitch in pig's tail,
Indian Pink
French knot in engine,
Black

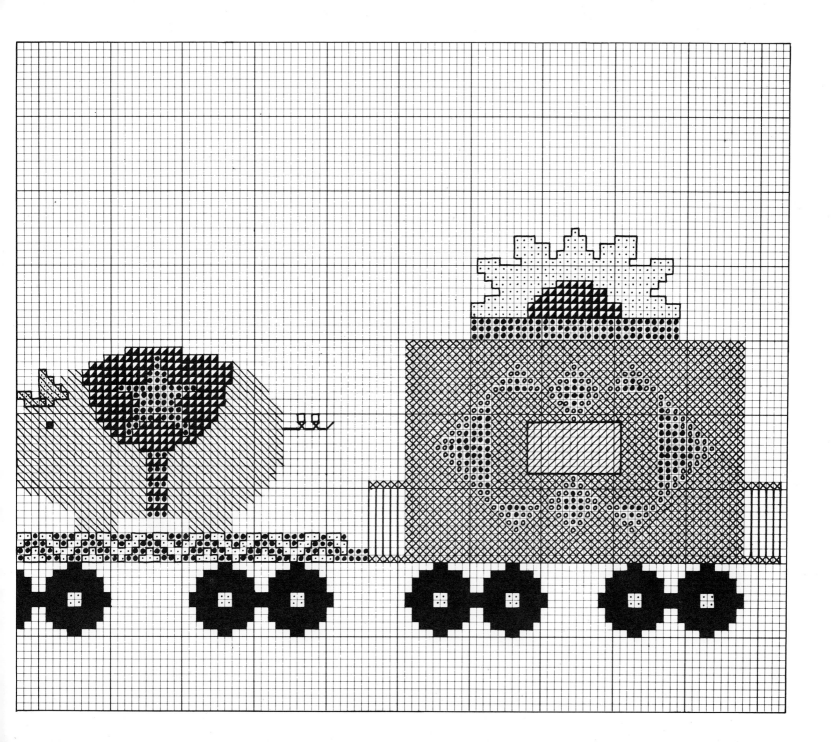

Chevrolet Coupe
Suggested fabric: Aida
cloth

☒ Steel Blue   108
☒ Tropic Orange   75-A
☒ Bright Gold   90-A
Ⅲ Charcoal   211
■ Black   12

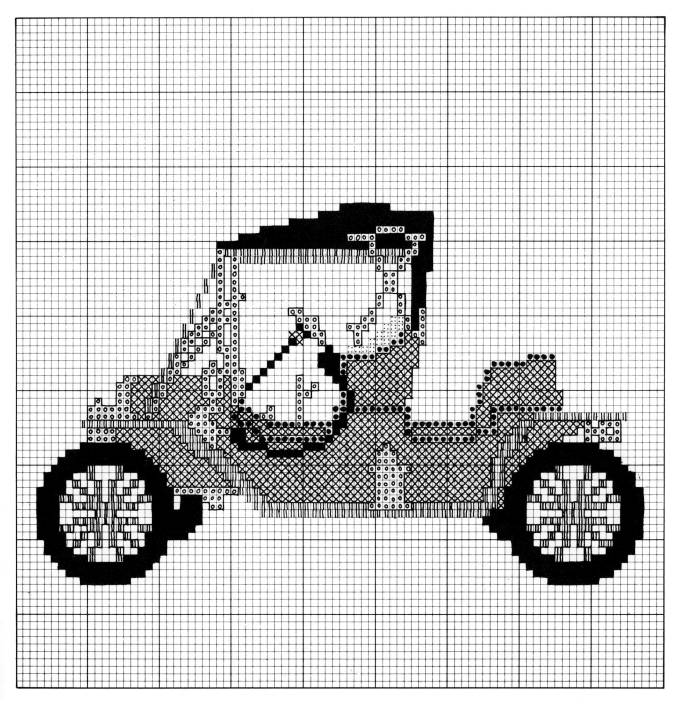

Model T Ford
Suggested fabric: Aida
cloth
⊡ Bright Gold 90-A
⊠ Tropic Orange 75-A
Ⅲ Charcoal 211
⊙ Colonial Brown 81-A
⊞ Blue Iris 221
■ Black 12

Army Air Corps

Suggested fabric: Aida
cloth or rug canvas

⊡ Blue 8
☐ White 1
☒ Steel Blue 108
■ Light Steel Blue 69
▨ Dark Orange 38
⊟ Bright Gold 90-A
⊞ Mid Pink 4-A
◉ Signal Red 140

French knot stitch for eye
in bird, Bright Gold
Outline stitch in face and
wheel, Steel Blue

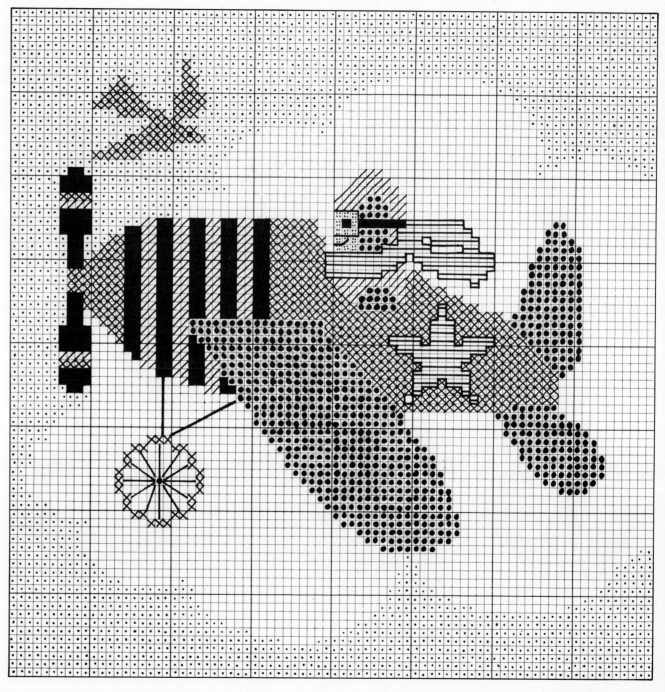

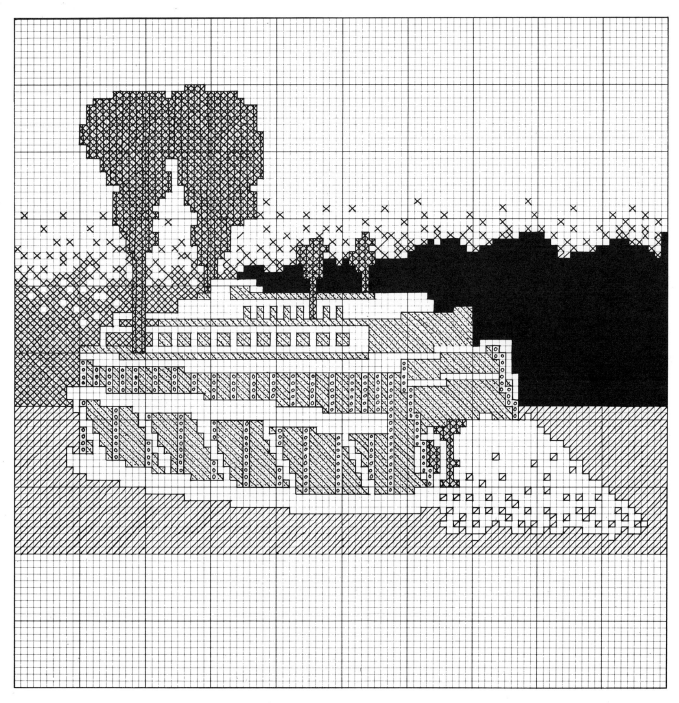

Mississippi Riverboat

Suggested fabric: Aida cloth

- ■ Dark Willow Green 109
- ☒ Bluette 220
- ◪ Silver Grey 70
- ⊡ Bright Gold 90-A
- ▨ Charcoal 211
- ◩ Royal Blue 44

Li'l Orphan Annie

Suggested fabric: Aida cloth

- ■ Signal Red 140
- ◉ Black 12
- □ White 1
- ⊡ Mid Pink 4-A
- ⊠ Dark Colonial Brown 81-B
- ◪ Gold Brown 51-C
- ◪ Tropic Orange 75-A

Outline stitch, Black

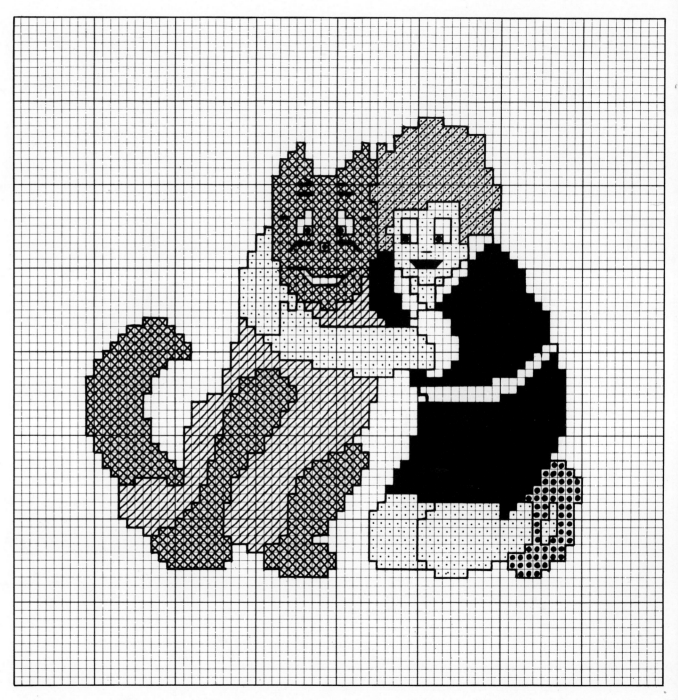

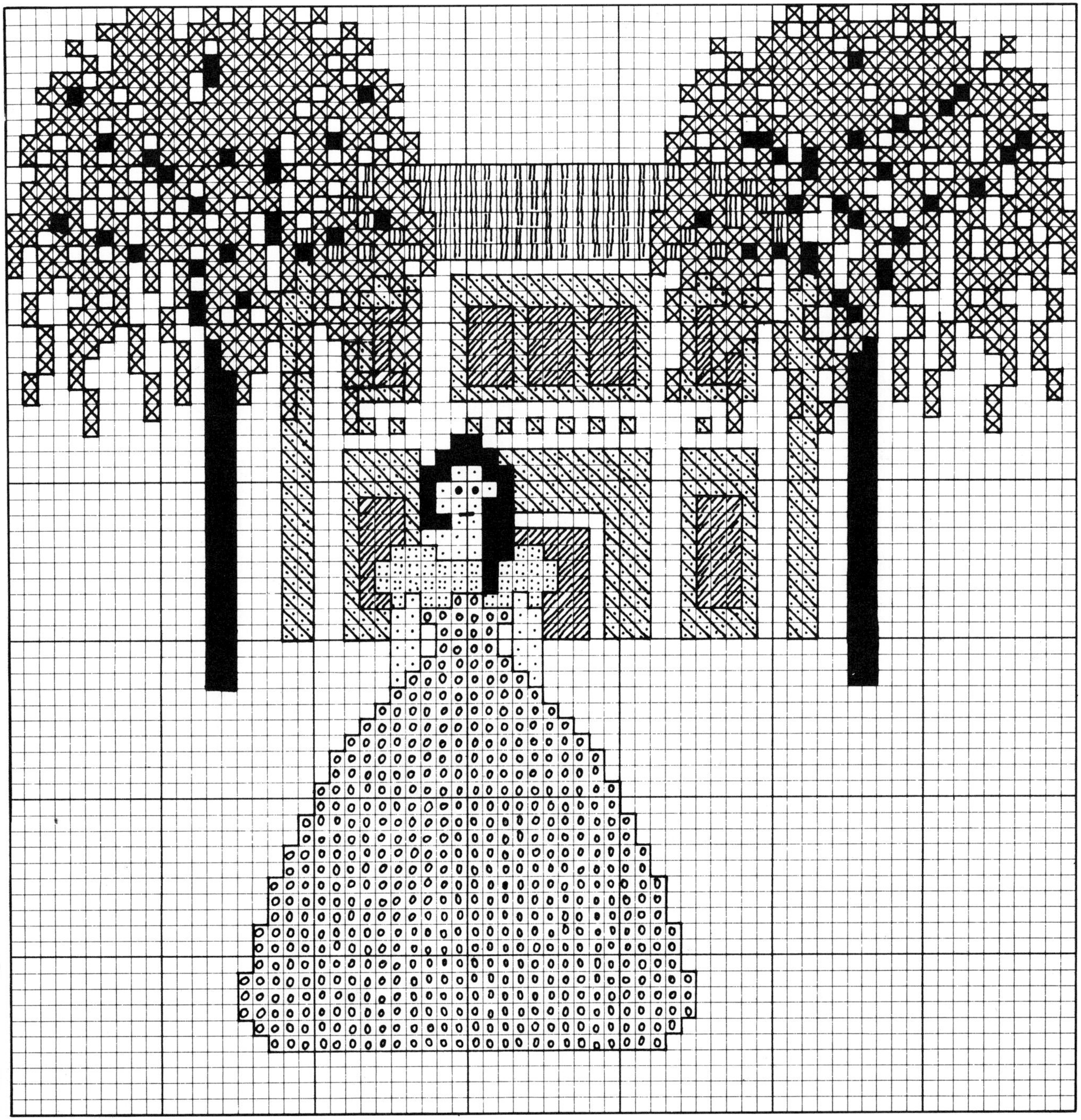

Southern Belle

Suggested fabric: Aida cloth

- ■ Colonial Brown 81-A
- ☒ Treeleaf Green 28-B
- ▨ Charcoal 211
- ⧅ Silver Grey 70
- ▥ Fast Red 100
- ⁘ Mid Rose 46-A
- ◙ Deep Rose 59-A
- ⊡ Ecru 61

Outline stitch for mouth, Deep Rose

French knots for eyes, Colonial Brown

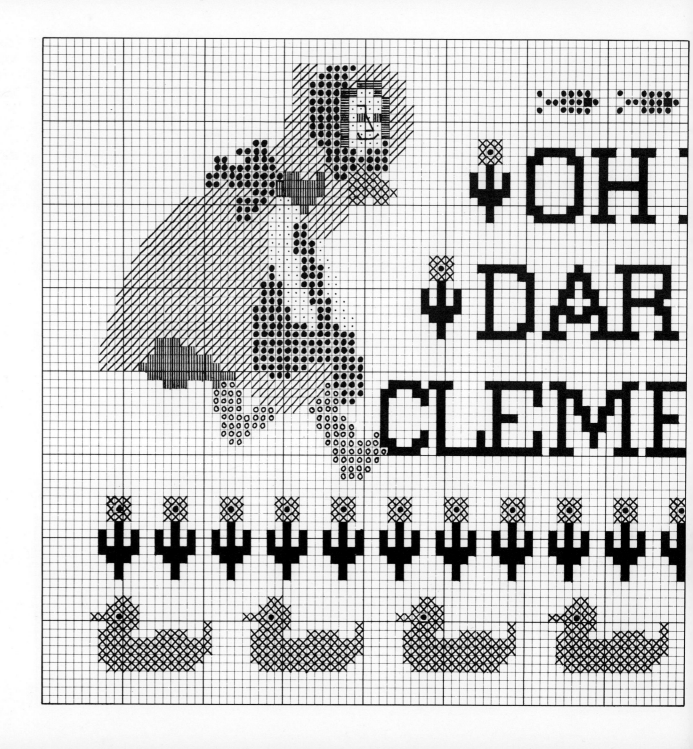

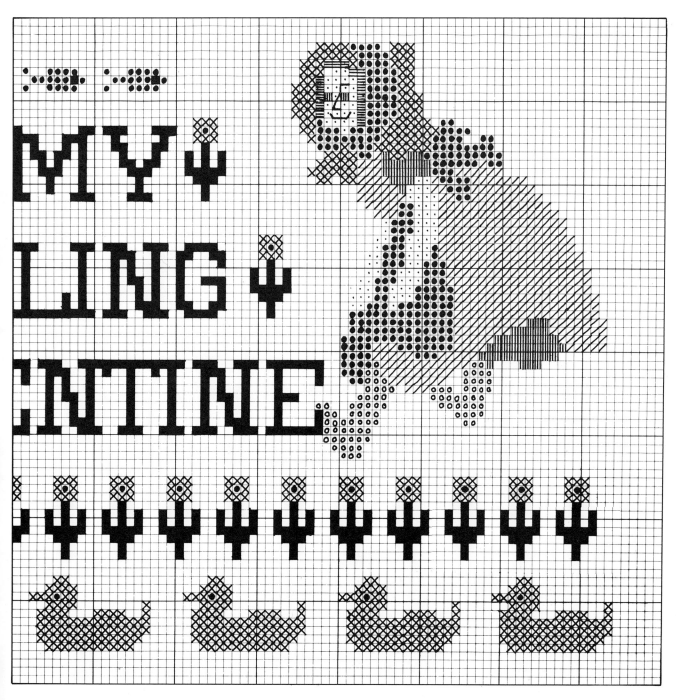

Oh My Darling, Clementine

Suggested fabric: Aida cloth

⊠ Sun Gold 223
■ Avocado 216
⊙ Dark Orange 38
▥ Blue Iris 221
⧄ Bluette 220
⊡ Mid Pink 4-A
▤ Gold Brown 51-C
◙ Dark Colonial Brown 81-B

Outline stitch in faces, Dark Colonial Brown

California Mission
Suggested fabric: Aida cloth

⊡ Indian Pink   124
☒ Gold Brown   51-C
⊙ Tropic Orange   75-A
■ Dark Colonial Brown 81-B
▨ Blue Iris   221
▥ Avocado   216
▨ Grass Green   99

Southwestern Indian Borders

Suggested fabric: Aida cloth or rug canvas

- ■ Black 12
- ▥ Signal Red 140
- ⊠ Charcoal 211
- ◪ Tangerine 38-B
- ⊡ Ecru 61
- □ White 1
- ◉ Tropic Orange 75-A

Indian Borders
Suggested fabric: Aida cloth
■ Black   12
◪ Signal Red   140
⊠ Steel Blue   108
⊡ Bright Gold   90-A

Zia Sun

Suggested fabric: rug
canvas

■ Tangerine   38-B
⊡ China Blue   76

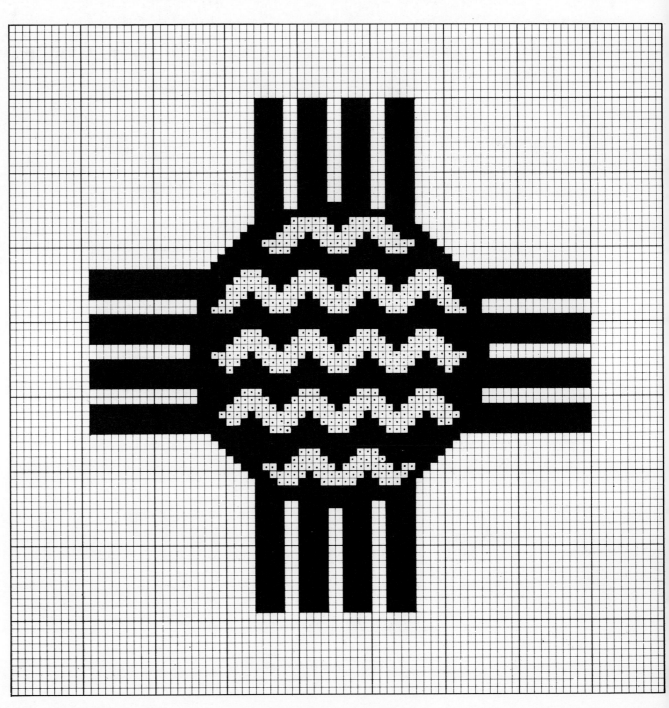

Navajo Diamonds

Suggested fabric: rug canvas

- ■ Navy 55
- ⊠ Signal Red 140
- □ Dark Yellow 43

Navajo Chief Blanket
Suggested fabric: Aida cloth or rug canvas
- ■ Black 12
- □ White 1
- ☒ Signal Red 140
- ◪ Royal Blue 44

Outline stitch in diamonds, Royal Blue

Southwestern Indian Twill
Suggested fabric: rug
canvas
☐ Royal Purple   36
☒ Tangerine   38-B
■ Signal Red   140

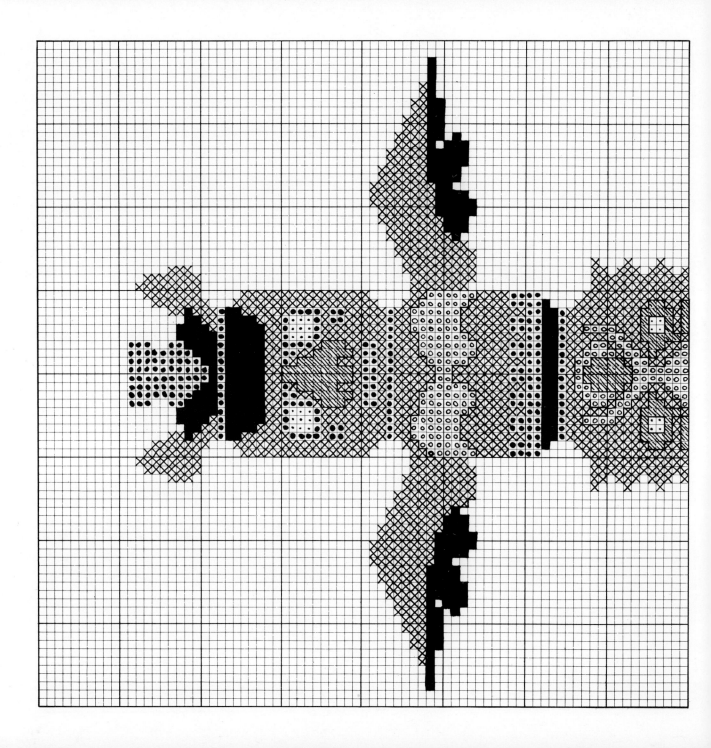

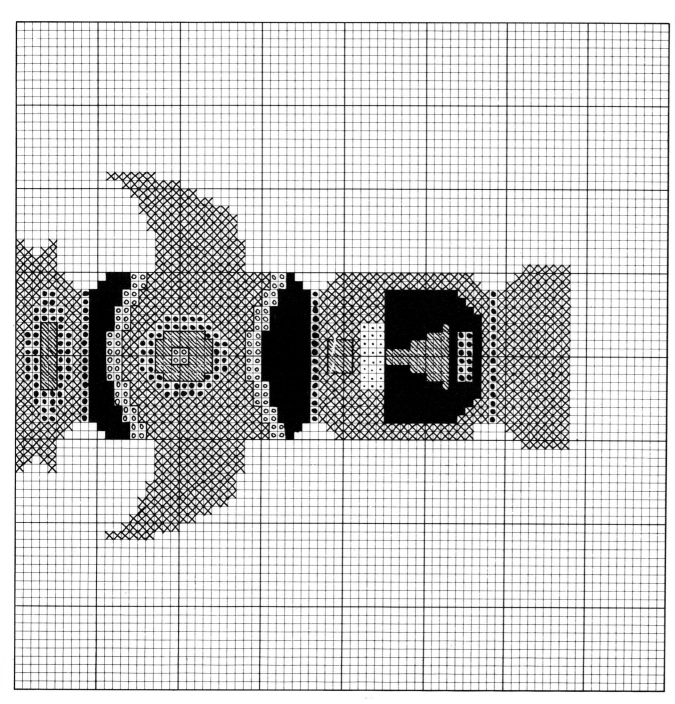

Totem Pole

Suggested fabric: Aida cloth

☒ Charcoal   211
◉ Fast Red   100
■ Treeleaf Green   28-B
◙ Bright Gold   90-A
▨ Tropic Orange   75-A
⊡ Steel Blue   108

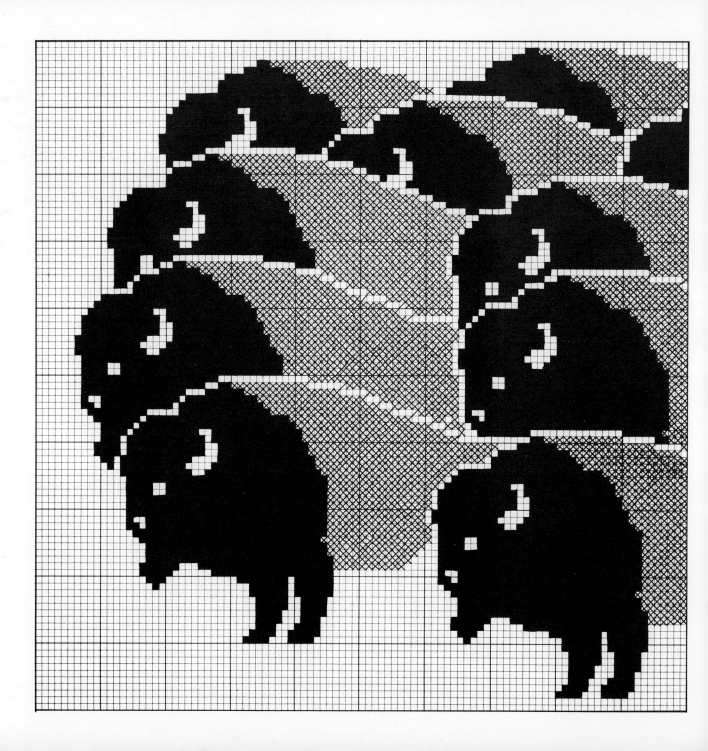

Buffalo
Suggested fabric: Aida cloth

⊠ Gold Brown   51-C

■ Dark Colonial Brown 81-B

Frontier Man
Indian Hunter
Suggested fabric: Aida cloth
⊠ Warm Beige 214
⊙ Bright Gold 90-A
⊡ Indian Pink 124
⊘ Gold Brown 51-C
⦿ Dark Colonial Brown 81-B
✳ Black 12
Ⅲ Signal Red 140
⊟ Tropic Orange 75-A
French knot for eyes, Steel Blue

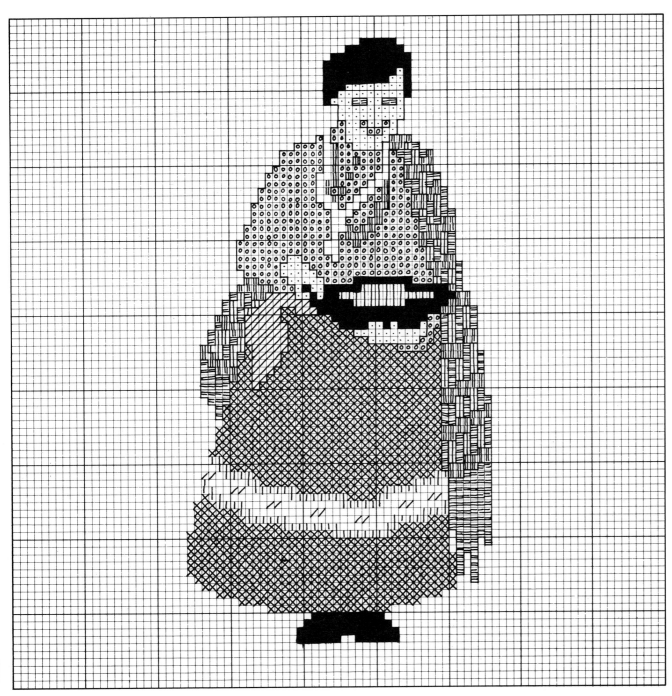

Navajo Indian Woman
Suggested fabric: Aida cloth

- ☒ Blue Iris   221
- ⊡ Indian Pink   124
- ⊙ Deep Rose   59-A
- ⊞ Sun Gold   223
- ⊟ Tropic Orange   75-A
- ☰ Royal Blue   44
- ☑ Leaf Green   210
- ■ Black   12

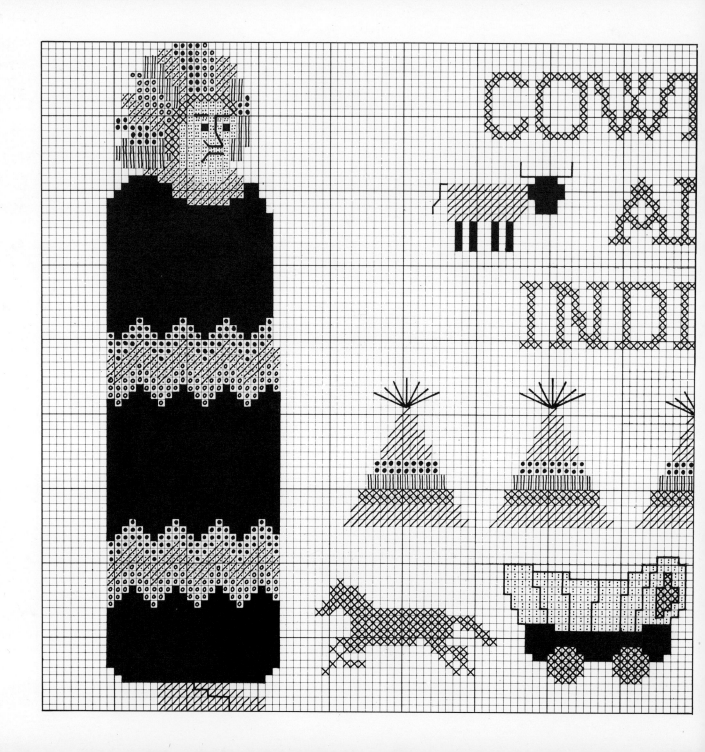

Cowboys and Indians

Suggested fabric: Aida cloth

- ■ Gold Brown 51-C
- ▨ Dark Colonial Brown 81-B
- ⫴ Signal Red 140
- ⊠ Black 12
- ⊙ Tangerine 38-B
- ⊡ Indian Pink 124
- ⊞ Tropic Orange 75-A
- ▨ Avocado 216
- ⊟ Blue 8
- ⊙ China Blue 76
- ⊡ Ecru 61

Outline stitch in faces, Dark Colonial Brown

Horse and Rider

Suggested fabric: Aida cloth

⊠ Gold Brown   51-C
⊡ Bright Gold   90-A
Ⅲ Beige   213
⧅ Signal Red   140
■ Black   12
⊞ Colonial Brown   81-A
⧄ Blue Iris   221

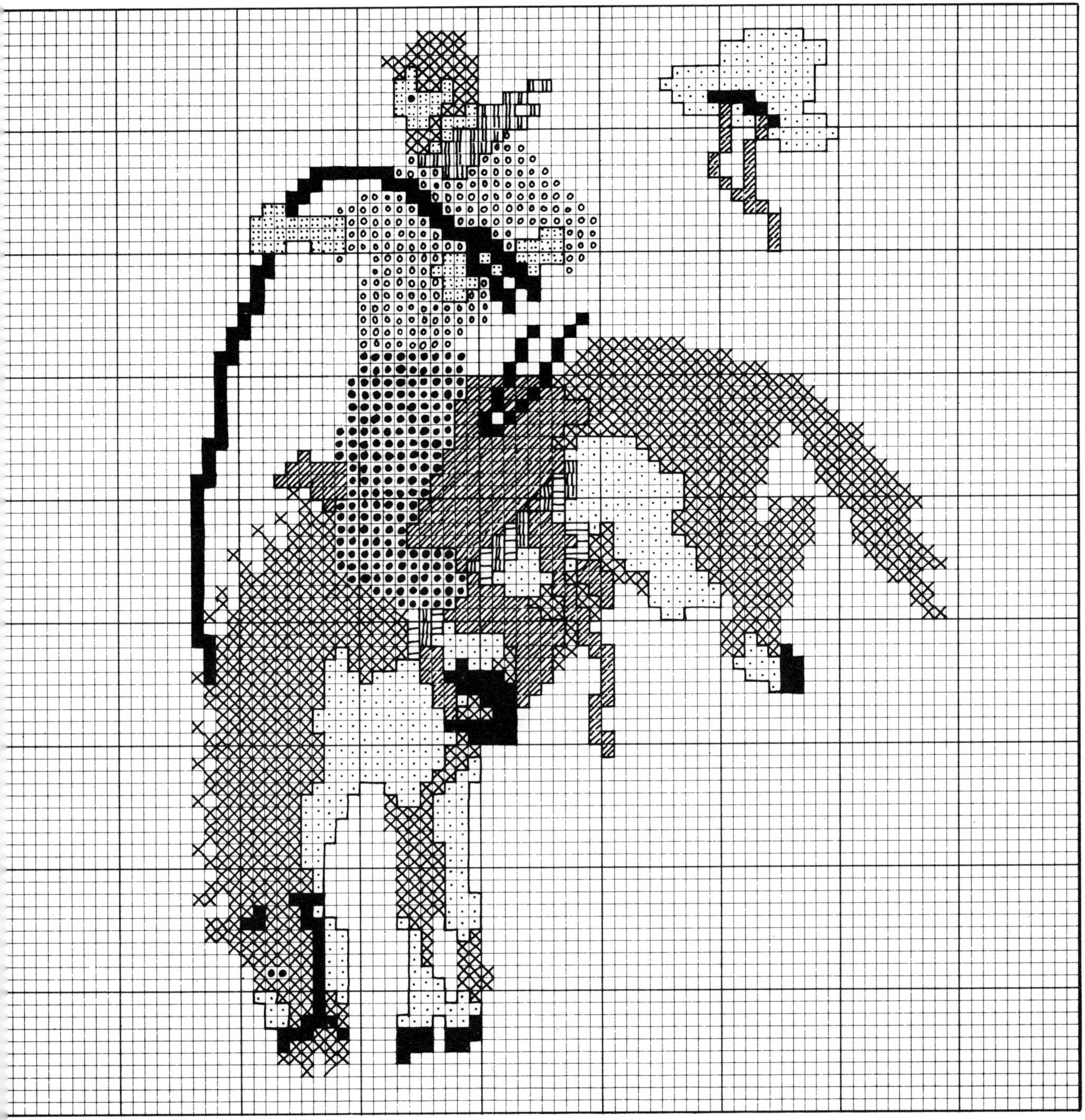

Bronco

Suggested fabric: Aida cloth

- ☒ Gold Brown 51-C
- ⊡ Bright Gold 90-A
- ◙ Royal Blue 44
- ▨ Colonial Brown 81-A
- ◎ Blue Iris 221
- ⚃ Indian Pink 124
- ▥ Signal Red 140
- ■ Black 12
- ⊟ Dark Orange 38

**Texas Longhorn
Campfire**

Suggested fabric: Aida
cloth

◫ Beige 213
▨ Dark Brown 81
■ Black 12
Ⅲ Tangerine 38-B
◉ Grass Green 99
⊠ Charcoal 211

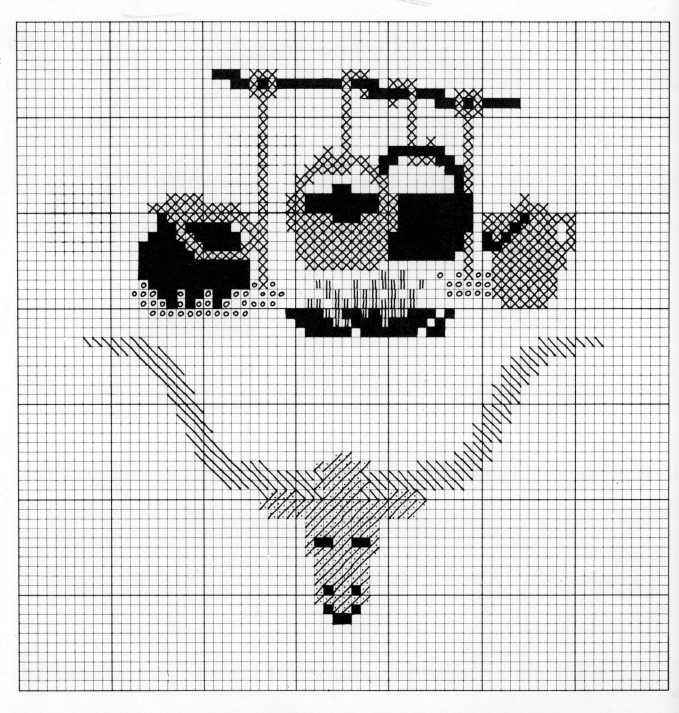

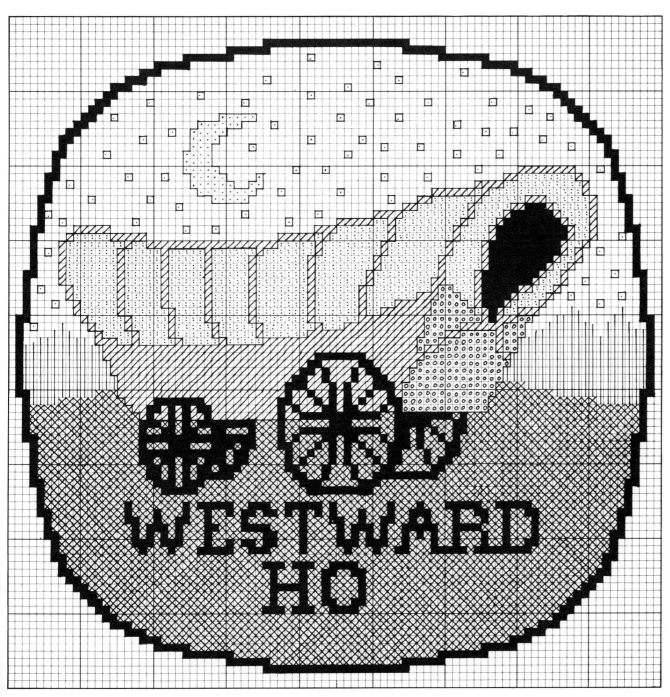

Westward Ho
Suggested fabric: Aida cloth

⊞ Purple 32
☑ Charcoal 211
■ Navy 55
☒ Treeleaf Green 28-B
⊡ Sun Gold 223
⊡ Ecru 61
◉ Pewter Grey 71

Western Twilight

Suggested fabric: Aida
cloth or rug canvas

Ⅲ Tangerine 38-B
Ⅱ Light Steel Blue 69
☐ Blue Iris 221
⊡ Royal Blue 44
☒ Royal Purple 36
■ Black 12
◪ Treeleaf Green 28-B